AF663529

Windows of Opportunity

Windows of Opportunity

Memoirs of an Economic Adviser

K. S. Krishnaswamy

Orient BlackSwan

in association with

SAMEEKSHA TRUST

ORIENT BLACKSWAN PRIVATE LIMITED

Registered Office
3-6-752 Himayatnagar, Hyderabad 500 029 (A.P.), India
Email: centraloffice@orientblackswan.com

Other Offices
Bangalore/Bhopal/Bhubaneshwar
Chennai/Ernakulam/Guwahati/Hyderabad/Kolkata
Jaipur/Lucknow/Mumbai/New Delhi/Patna

© K. S. Krishnaswamy

Cover design
© Orient Blackswan Private Limited 2010

First Published 2010

ISBN 978-81-250-3964-8

Printed at
Graphica Printers
Hyderabad 500 013

Published by
Orient Blackswan Private Limited
3-6-752 Himayatnagar, Hyderabad 500 029 (A.P.), India
Email: hyderabad@orientblackswan.com

To
my wife Madhura,
and
Bansi and Vikram
for their love and support

CONTENTS

ACKNOWLEDGEMENTS

MEMBERS of my generation have benefited much from the many opportunities that became available after Independence. This is an account of my experiences in that context. I have set them down in the hope that it may persuade others to do so, so that some individual accounts may enrich India's economic history.

In writing this I have referred often to two major publications which became available to me recently: the three-volume history of the Reserve Bank of India published in 2005 as a set by that institution, and Ramachandra Guha's *India since Gandhi* which came out in 2007. They have saved me from committing several egregious errors of fact or sequence. I wish to acknowledge my debt to them.

I have benefited much from comments and suggestions from family members and friends who were kind enough to read the first draft. These include, besides my own family, my brother Dr K S Srinivas and my nephews, Shivakumar and K N Arun. Among my friends, I wish to thank Drs Ashok Mitra, A Vaidyanathan, Rammanohar Reddy and Ms Meenakshi Thyagarajan. Unfortunately I have not been able to consult with Dr K N Raj because of his ill-health; nor pay my debt to a late brother-in-law who had long urged me to write my memoirs.

The preparation of this volume has been greatly assisted by R Thyagarajan and his associates in the Centre for Budgetary Policy and Studies in Bangalore and by the editor and his colleagues in the *Economic and Political Weekly* in Mumbai. Without their cooperation, it would not have been possible for me to bring this out quickly. I wish to record my gratitude to all of them.

Bangalore
December 2009

K S Krishnaswamy

ABBREVIATIONS

ARDC	Agricultural Refinance and Development Corporation
BCCI	Bank of Credit and Commerce International
CAS	Credit Authorisation Scheme
CPC	Credit Planning Cell
CPI	Communist Party of India
CRR	Cash Reserve Ratio
CSO	Central Statistical Organisation
DBOD	Department of Banking Operations and Development
DRI	Differential Rate of Interest
ECAFE	Economic Commission for Asia and the Far East
EDI	Economic Development Institute
FCI	Food Corporation of India
FEDIND	Federation of Indian Student's Associations
ICICI	Industrial Credit and Investment Corporation of India
ICS	Indian Civil Service
IDA	International Development Association
IDBI	Industrial Development Bank of India
IEA	Indian Economic Association
IFCI	Industrial Finance Corporation of India
IMF	International Monetary Fund
ISI	Indian Statistical Institute
LIC	Life Insurance Corporation of India
LSE	London School of Economics
MIT	Massachusetts Institute of Technology
NDC	National Development Council
NIBM	National Institute of Bank Management
NIU	National Income Unit
NSIC	National Small Industries Corporation
NSSO	National Sample Survey Organisation
PC	Planning Commission
PMO	Prime Minister's Office
PRIS	Panchayat Raj Institutions
RBI	Reserve Bank of India
RCI	Refinance Corporation for Industry
RRBs	Regional Rural Banks
SBI	State Bank of India
SDR	Special Drawing Rights
SFC	State Finance Corporation
SLR	Statutory Liquidity Ratio
SSA	Sarva Shiksha Abhiyan
UNCTAD	United Nations Committee on Trade and Development
USES	University's School of Economics and Sociology
UTI	Unit Trust of India

Preamble

"All you have are significant remains of one kind or another. You can extrapolate backward, but that is dangerous."

–Joseph Campbell (1988): *The Power of Myth*, p 71.

I have often wondered at the clarity with which some are able to recall their past. Not just some unusual or traumatic experience. But a whole series of events they have lived through, with every little detail. They seem to remember where exactly they were, with whom and when, the dresses they were wearing, the food they ate and even the colour and smell of the houses, gardens, fields or farms around them. More amazingly, they can recount the thoughts that crossed their minds scores of years ago or the emotions they felt, as if they were talking about yesterday.

How do they do it? Are they really endowed with some special faculties of remembrance and retrieval? Or, are they romanticising their past, shifting a good bit of the present into the past, and telescoping many things into a short-span experience in such a way as to make a good story? Whatever the reason, I truly envy them. Every time I try to visualise my early days, a series of disjointed pictures float across the mind's eye with vague persons, bits of dialogue, a medley of tastes and smells, and no clear notion of how it all began or ended. Perhaps, my early days were indeed a medley, not half as lively or eventful as some other people's were, or my memory and retrieval mechanisms are weak. Either way, I do not qualify for delving into the past to relive my early years through an autobiographic essay.

Why then am I engaged in this task of remembrance? If, as psychologists say, more than half of what I am today is determined by the environment and experience of my childhood, I cannot really know why I am what I am or the premises of my current philosophy, without going back in time all the way to my childhood. Maybe that is going too far, considering that the sum total of one's experience – including reading, observing, doing and reasoning – are far more a part of adult rather than childhood years. True enough, by the time you are an adolescent, you already carry ideas, images and impressions in a virgin brain; and memories that are stored thereafter are filtered or modified by a "censor" that has somehow come to be the subconscious of the child. But is this censor immutable? Do not later experiences alter it in some way? Reason dictates that we do not rule out this possibility. Though as T S Eliot says, time past and time future are both in time present, it seems clear that time past does not wholly determine time present.

When I sit down to trace the roots of my being, I am in effect filtering the past through the present. I select some as relevant or important or significant because I feel now that it is so. That at any rate is what I have done here. Of the innumerable things that happened in my formative years, I have dwelt on only those which, on reflection today and in the light of my present values and complexes, I believe have contributed to my development and character. Some of these concern me; others relate to the circumstances of life in those days which in my present understanding were a significant influence on young minds. These may be conditions of family life, social obligations, political or cultural events or anything else having one common characteristic – they were all part of a way of life which has become a bygone era for the generations of today. They are, in other words, a part of history in themselves and not because of any connection with me; they had a part in moulding me rather than the other way round. I can truthfully relate them without feeling that in so doing, I am packaging myself in any way.

One more detail before I start. Most of my formative years were spent in an India which was struggling to gain independence, led by Mahatma Gandhi, Jawaharlal Nehru and other leaders of the Indian National Congress. Among the many conundrums I began to wonder about in my youth a constant one was whether there was any connection between the poverty of India and the affluence of India's political masters, between political dependence and economic backwardness. These were not phrases or expressions that were known to me, much less understood by me in my school days. But much more than science and its wonders, these were questions that seemed worth studying in later years. This interest in economic, social and political inter-relationships has persisted over the years; perhaps that is why this account of my past is woven around a connecting thread of economic transformations during the last 60 years or so. Fortunately for me, independent India gave those of my generation unbelievable opportunities to participate in the exciting endeavour of trying to transform a country steeped in tradition and impoverished by economic exploitation. In our age of innocence and faith, we had little doubt that independence, democracy, social justice, and the scientific spirit would go hand in hand with economic progress. We did not then have the benefit of hindsight. The balance between material betterment and the non-economic values essential for the preservation of social health has naturally varied from time to time since the late 1940s. But despite the growth of commercialism, an exploitative bureaucracy and political opportunism, it is astonishing that there should have been, throughout these years, concern for quality, ethical values, environmental protection, in a word, for the quality of common life in India. Granted that often times, these have been patently deceptive. But the fallout of even such selfish actions has been beneficial to some extent. In reliving my past, I am trying to explain to myself the how and why of this phenomenon. If it adds a little to the understanding of others, or at least raises pertinent questions about India's recent social history, I am more than content.

1

Early Years

I

THERE is not much that I can remember very exciting about my early childhood. My brother (who was a couple of years older than me) and I spent our days mostly in or near the house. My father, Kadur Shamanna, was a sub-assistant surgeon in the medical service of the state of Mysore, posted in a taluq headquarters. We lived in a modest house across the street from my father's dispensary, which we could visit only occasionally, under the care of a servant. The dispensary was not by any means large and catered only for outpatients. But it constituted our entire concept of a "hospital". Apart from catching a glimpse of our father at work, the attraction for us was the large compound in which we could play without hindrance when the sun was not severe.

In those years, the early 1920s, there were no play schools even in towns bigger than the one in which we lived. My brother had been enrolled in the government primary school, which I was too young to attend. However my parents and grandmother had decided that I could not afford to delay education too long, and was taught the Kannada alphabet and numbers at home. My brother and I also had to learn the short prayers that were customarily recited in a brahmin household. Some evenings, the compounder of my father's dispensary would come to tell us stories from the *Panchatantra*, *Ramayana*, and *Mahabharata*. He was a kindly old gentleman who added to his meagre salary through such means, or by officiating as a priest during the innumerable festivals that my parents were wont to observe. I also remember his staying on some evenings to teach my father how to play the violin. To our joy we were allowed to sit in on these sessions and perhaps our subconscious benefited from it. We have enjoyed listening to good music in later years, though neither of us studied it systematically.

As I came to recognise some years later, government officers enjoyed much authority and respect in those days. My father's responsibility, like those of his colleagues in other services, extended far beyond the town and the hospital, to all the villages and people in the taluq. Besides the daily routine of treating outpatients at the dispensary, he had to go round the town regularly, to visit the very sick in their houses or check on suspected cases of cholera and other communicable diseases. He had also to visit, on request or on his own, the many villages in the taluq, as doctor and public health officer. This was particularly frequent when there was an outbreak of an epidemic in the vicinity and people had to be immunised. Since he was on the payroll of the state government, he was not entitled to any fees for such visits; but it was apparently the custom those days for the beneficiaries to show their gratitude in some concrete form – gold or silver coins, a bag of rice, ragi or a basket of fruits, vegetables or coconuts, a pot of ghee or butter, at least a garland and a couple of limes. The more affluent of his patients sometimes brought a sari for my mother or a silver cup for the children on special occasions. We did not, of course, understand the ethics of this custom; but whenever my father went on a village visit or was taken urgently by somebody to see a sick patient, we used to look forward to his returning with some goodies for the house.

Travel was not easy, nor the occasions for travel many. When he went on his village visits or to the district headquarters to meet senior officers, he travelled by bus or bullock cart. Because of his official status, he was always accorded the special privilege of occupying the front seat to the left of the driver. Buses those days were not too many or well designed and tended invariably to be overcrowded. However, the front seat provided relief to at least two people and was much sought after by the passengers when it was not reserved for local VIPs. It was also considered appropriate for the bus to come to the house or to the dispensary to pick up my father before starting out on the journey. On the rare occasions when my father took the family out to the district headquarters for a visit or to Bangalore or Mysore, an entire row in the forward portion of the bus would be reserved for us. If those who were crowded into the less comfortable rear seats disliked this, they did not show it and, in any event, we were too young to be concerned about other people's rights and privileges. In retrospect, I believe in those days, everybody accepted such privileges for government servants as in some way natural. Kings and zamindars (landlords) had always taken whatever they liked, regardless of the rights or needs of others; this authority had continued under the Mughals and the British. Mysore was still a principality and for his subjects, the maharaja was the incarnation of divine authority; hence his "servants" enjoyed a special status.

Despite all economic and political changes since then, this attitude continues, especially among government officers at all levels. From *gram sevaks* (secretaries to village panchayats) to secretaries to the Government of India, and ministers and legislators, public functionaries have appropriated for themselves a variety of privileges which bear little relation to their needs or responsibilities. There is, of course, a greater awareness of the inequity implicit in this now, when government employees are paid very much more than in my father's days. But in those times of little education, much poverty and authoritarian regimes, even the thought of being discriminated against was foreign to most people. It was all their karma.

By the time I was five, my father was transferred to a somewhat smaller station, a sub-taluq in the hilly tracts along the western part of the state. This was part of his service obligation, to complete a certain number of years in Malnad. His new posting was a hardship station, heavy with rainfall and malaria. The town was less than 16 kilometres to the west of the district headquarters, stretching ribbon-like along the road to the port town of Mangalore on the Arabian Sea. To the west of the town, scrub jungle progressively developed into lush forests and coffee plantations on the distant hill-slopes. My father's jurisdiction extended mostly towards villages in this direction.

My brother was soon to enter middle school and as there was only a primary school in the town, my father decided to send him to Bangalore. I was admitted to the local school, which was conveniently located across the street from our house. The headmaster of the school was a distant relation on my mother's side, which was both an advantage and a curse. He kept a constant eye on me when I was at school and often crossed over to our house on social visits. Though not a harsh man, he had a loud voice and I never could make out if he was asking me something or ordering me.

I have only a few memories of those years in the primary school. I believe I was a good student and do not remember to have been punished in any manner. But I was frequently laid low with malaria as indeed all the others in the family or at school. Together with my small build, this debilitating disease seriously restricted my extra-curricular activities. Several of my friends would frequently venture into the forests around town, looking for fruits and berries of various kinds or hoping to catch a glimpse of some wild animal or bird. For the most part, they did it on the sly. I missed many such after-school jaunts, often because of malaria, but sometimes because my friends told me brutally that I could not cope. This sense of physical inadequacy has persisted over the years, and has been a significant cause of my inability to be aggressive even when I disapprove strongly of somebody or something.

During a little over three years in that town, my father took us a few times out on what were then long journeys by bus or train. Some of these were to the state's largest city, Bangalore, and others to Mysore, where the maharaja lived. I believe that our visits to Mysore were later, since I can recall a little of the details of visits to the palace, which was awesome, and the zoo, which was a delight. During one of these visits, my father had to be hospitalised and the family had some anxious moments. This was the first time that I saw a real hospital, with numerous wards and scores of doctors and nurses scurrying around in their white aprons. But the journey that most often comes back to me is the pilgrimage to a holy place in the coastal district of South Kanara. I am not certain whether this came after my father's hospitalisation, by way of fulfilment of a vow taken by my grandmother or mother; but it clearly had the purpose of propitiating the serpent god Subramanya. We travelled by bus, crossing the Western Ghats on a road of steep gradients, hair-pin bends and glorious forest all around. Accidents on this road were quite common, especially during the monsoon when landslides and fog occurred rather suddenly. The great trees covering the steep hill sides along which the road traversed remains an evergreen memory, despite my being sick on the bus. Many years later, when my wife and I travelled by car up the ghats from the coastal side, the denudation that had occurred in the name of progress and development was sickening. The memory of the lush forest I had seen several decades ago came back to me – disturbing and yet oddly comforting.

The shrine where our family had to offer prayers was beautifully located beside a river. It had the reputation of being a "powerful" shrine, capable of harming those who entered without bathing in the river and discarding their work clothes. Along with my grandmother and parents, my sisters and I were also given a bath and taken into the temple in wet clothes. We did not mind it, for the weather was congenial and moreover, we were terrified that otherwise we would be attacked by cobras wherever we went. It was also obligatory for the worshippers to fast until the rituals were over and any special penance which they had vowed was done. On that day, my grandmother rolled on the ground from the main door of the temple to the sanctum sanctorum. I do not remember whether my mother and father also did so, but there were many other devotees doing so. There was a feast in the temple in which all those who had offered puja (ritual worship) were to participate. This was a special occasion; we were told that after the food was served, we had to refrain from eating until the lord of the temple, the king of cobras, passed along the aisle and entered his abode behind the idol. We did not see any cobra slide along where we sat, but we waited with considerable trepidation and were indeed relieved when it was announced a little later that the lord had indeed blessed us and reached home.

In that temple as in many others, brahmins controlled not merely the puja procedures but everything else – for instance, who could worship and who could not or who could enter the inner precinct. Those belonging to other castes were not allowed into the inner court during the morning service, nor could they sit to eat alongside the brahmins. None of this was, of course, part of my cognition at that time and as children we had no inkling of the enormous power of brahmins in the community. We took it as part of the natural order that we were superior, purer than others and of a higher order. The astonishing part of it was that others also seemed to accept our assumption of this higher status. They did not allow it to spoil personal relationships, and never invited us to eat with them. Not only did they not object to eating in our house, but felt no hurt when they were served separately and even required to clean the place where they had eaten. But it was not long before all these things changed.

II

By the time my father was transferred to his next station, I had passed the third standard in the primary school. I had done well in the examinations and the headmaster recommended to my father that I be admitted to the first level in the middle school at the place to which we moved. With my father's position as the local doctor and my school record, this posed no major problem. But some of the teachers were not pleased, nor were some of my classmates. There were also a couple of subjects with which I could not cope easily. When in the class tests held a few months later, I did poorly in these subjects, my class teacher made me stand up on the bench for public ridicule – as a punishment for claiming privileges beyond my capability. The teachers were obviously right in objecting to my jumping a year on the basis of what they considered an undue favour. But the hurt to me was great, and I recall with gratitude the kindness with which a few of my classmates treated me on that day. In the final examination that year, I topped the class in all but English composition, and the teachers who had upbraided me earlier were most appreciative, compensating for the bitterness caused earlier.

My father's tenure in that town was long enough for me to complete my high-school education. Those years were not only satisfying from the viewpoint of academic progress but also exciting in many ways. The town was in an arid zone, and lay at the foot of a hill, which had been fortified in the past by a minor warlord. A large part of the fort surrounding the hill remained intact, though the fortifications and buildings on the hill had been ruined during one of the many wars between the rulers of old Mysore, the Bahmani kings, the Marathas and the European colonisers. The top part of the hill was a large rock massif, with a few narrow steps cut into it. Adjoining this hill were minor hillocks covered like the base of the hill with shrubs and tall grass. Besides a variety of berries and wild fruit, this scrub jungle reputedly abounded in cobras, minor game, poachers and bootleggers and other mysterious individuals practising strange and terrible things. Altogether, it was exciting for us to climb these hills in search of fruit or just for the fun of it. However, we were timid enough to get out of the woods well before nightfall, and avoided them altogether when the town was rife with rumours about a ferocious leopard sighted in the vicinity.

Besides these forays, life within and outside school was also rich with new experiences. Till we left high school, all students had to study English and a second language, world geography, some Indian history, and the rudiments of physics, chemistry, biology, algebra, geometry and trigonometry. We had for the most part good teachers who knew their subjects well enough to inform us more than what was required in the syllabus. I remember being fascinated by the practical demonstrations in physics and chemistry, the novelty of algebraic operations, the mysteries of biology and not least by the vistas of English and Kannada literature that my teachers opened for us. It was still an age to learn and wonder rather than analyse and question. We were beginning to see that the world around us was immense, enormously variegated, and beautiful beyond compare. It was many years before I could see that there was also much cruelty and ugliness in this world of ours.

But for the moment, the sense of well-being dominated during class hours, and was enhanced later by the opportunities available on the playing fields. The school was not, of course, rich enough to provide a swimming pool or tennis courts. But thanks to a headmaster who was a sports enthusiast, there were enough facilities for all the students to play football, volleyball, badminton or cricket, or go for physical exercises in the gymnasium. Several of the teachers also participated in these activities, often to our amusement. My brother, who had come home from Bangalore and joined the high school, excelled at football and badminton. I was not much good at any, though I played all of them. By the time I left school, however, I had become a second string bowler in the cricket team and even travelled once to another town for an inter-school match.

While the school naturally dominated our lives, other experiences also accumulated. The town was the headquarters of a district sub-division; there were also the base-level civil and magistrate's courts, a full-fledged post and telegraph office, a police inspectorate, a sub-treasury and veterinary hospital, besides my father's dispensary. There were no banks, and I am not sure if there was a co-operative society, but there were a few substantial merchants and landlords who lent money. The town's elite corps of officers had formed a club, where they played tennis and card games in the evenings. The club was situated within the outer fort of the hill and remained pretty exclusive. Since my father was a member, we could go there occasionally to scan newspapers. Sometime before I completed school, my brother and some of his friends decided to organise a football team, probably because of differences with the captain of the school team. The club authorities allowed this group to use a field abutting the club grounds and some of the club members came along to play with us occasionally.

Neither the school nor the officer's club organised any cultural activities and we fell back on the town for this need. Two temples, one of Shiva and the other of Vishnu, dominated the town centre. Besides special worship during the many festivals observed by Hindus, there were events like *harikathas* (stories on religious themes) and *bhajan* (devotional music) parties which we could attend. Even more special than these were the touring circuses and dramatic troupes, which came to the town at least once every year, complete with their tents, performing animals, stage settings and above all, electricity generators and rows of colourful lights. As usual, all senior officers were special invitees to these shows. My father enjoyed such diversions and took us with him. These performances were a source of both enjoyment and education for us. A good bit of my knowledge of Indian mythology, romantic literature and ancient history was garnered from these recitations, *harikathas* and dramatic shows.

As I have mentioned earlier, my grandmother and parents were deeply religious. Observance of festivals and visits to the temples were frequent and we were expected to accompany them regardless of our interests or feelings. Many of these were also social gatherings, during which there was mass eating or singing. Most gatherings at home were limited to members of one's own caste, in our case, brahmins. However, there were some functions in which everybody participated—car festivals, Muharram, the annual *jatra* (folk theatre) and Navarathri festivities. Along the roads traversed by temple cars and *tazias* (representations of the tombs of Hasan and Hussain, the grandsons of the Prophet, carried in processions for various Islamic festivities), offerings were made by all communities. Even my grandmother offered prayers at a Muslim *darga* (shrine of a Sufi saint) during the Muharram festivities and when my mother organised a special display of decorated dolls during Navarathri, it was an open house for everybody. The annual *jatra* was something else. It was a combination of sacrificial offerings to the village deity and a large-scale fair. The latter was great fun with acrobats, magicians and numerous stalls selling clothes, pots and pans, oddments needed for farms or cattle, bangles of all kinds, fruits and vegetables and a variety of eatables and drinks. The ritual part of these *jatras* was, however, quite terrifying. These were mostly after sundown, accompanied by an incessant beating of drums and cymbals. The priests looked fierce in their yellow and red robes, paint and matted locks. Goats and chicken were sacrificed before the idol, which looked fierce, and devotees often broke into dance. The *jatra* reached a frenzied climax with the beheading of a sacrificial buffalo, fire walking by devotees in a semi-trance, the thunder of drums, breathless waiting for the deity's word of satisfaction, acrobatics on a high beam and revellers high on drugs and toddy. As the entire ritual centred on propitiating evil spirits, we were terrified for days thereafter and avoided going anywhere near the *jatra* grounds, lest some unsatisfied ghoul gobble us up.

By the time my father was transferred again, I had completed my high school and was ready to enter college. Luckily for me, he was posted to the big government hospital in Mysore, in which he had been a patient some years earlier. Unlike in other places where he was the chief medical officer, he was part of the junior staff of general practitioners in this hospital, servicing the outpatient department or doing duty in the wards. He was assigned one of the staff quarters within the hospital area, which though adequate was a far cry from the big houses and numerous perquisites to which we had become accustomed in the smaller towns. But all this was outweighed by the excitement of living in a city and joining the university.

III

This was a transition in more ways than one. The years in high school had opened up several vistas and generated new interests—literature and mythology, mathematics, cricket and, to some extent, history and economics. But I was still very much a frog in the well, happy in the limited environment of a privileged youngster in a small town. There was little awareness of the dimensions of society around me, its rigidities and limitations, its excellences and injustices. Though the late 1920s and early 1930s were years of momentous happenings in India's freedom struggle, I was barely aware of it all. Of course I had heard of Gandhi and had even read occasionally about his fasts and imprisonments. When I was still a middle-school student, some of the political activists in the town had marched in a procession to the school and urged us to come out in protest against something or the other. But I had no idea what it was all about. The doings of the Indian National Congress and its leaders were not familiar to me since they were not talked about either in school or at home. Whatever was happening was in the British provinces – outside the state of Mysore, where we owed allegiance to the maharaja and his government. Moreover, we had been trained at school to appreciate the greatness of the British Empire "on which the sun never sets". England was rich, mighty and the world leader in many respects. We were led to believe that its literature was the best, its universities the greatest temples of learning, it was unbeatable in cricket (until Don Bradman came along) and its people superior to others in every way. The only opportunity I had of reading newspapers was when my father brought them home from the club once in a while. I have also the feeling that because of his campaign for free admission of *harijans* (the lower castes) to Hindu temples, Gandhi had lost respect in most brahmin households and ours was no exception.

However, Gandhi's voyage to London for the Round Table Conference in 1931 left a deep impression on me and his doings there were one of the few non-sports items that I followed, though I understood little of its purpose or political content. It was uplifting to see him totally at ease wherever he went, relaxed and utterly confident. It was also a revelation for those of my generation that despite his steadfast refusal to toe the British line or wear a suit, Gandhi was greatly respected even in Europe. During those days, I frequently went to the officer's club for cricket news in *The Hindu*. I soon found myself reading about Gandhi, Nehru, Sardar Vallabhbhai Patel, C Rajagopalachari and other national leaders. Following Gandhi's arrest on his return to India, the civil disobedience movement gathered momentum and it was impossible not to become aware of the ruthless lathi charges and firing by the police all over India.

It was only after we shifted to Mysore that I got to know more about the how and why of these happenings. As soon as I joined the Intermediate College, I had access to the much bigger libraries of the college and the university. I had access also to the reading facilities at the university students' union which subscribed to a number of English newspapers and magazines. More important than these were the exposures to politically aware teachers and other older persons, some of whom had been satyagrahis (practitioners of non-violent resistance) in adjoining British provinces. One of the more important of such contacts for me was an older cousin of mine named K Ramaswami, who, though an engineering student in Bangalore, was an ardent follower of Gandhi and the national movement. It was in his father's house that my brother had stayed after joining college in Mysore, until my father's transfer there. This cousin was an excellent public speaker and debator, a bibliophile and a political activist. It was through his constant encouragement that my brother and I learnt a great deal more about the freedom movement. Besides Gandhi's autobiography, I became an avid reader of the *Harijan* and other publications that emanated from Gandhian or Congress sources which my cousin often lent me.

Other differences between school and college emerged. It was a considerable distance to the university and Mysore was too small to afford a city bus service. After a while both my brother and I acquired bicycles. We were also given pocket money for snacks and other incidental expenses. Besides cricket and outdoor games, facilities were provided in the university union building for table tennis, carom, chess and draughts. There was also a radio, which only designated individuals could operate in the evening. The radio was devoted almost entirely to listening to cricket scores and commentaries until Mussolini invaded Abyssinia and war news gained importance.

In addition to the union, there were numerous student associations organised for specific subjects as also others like the Rover Scouts Group and the drama society, which any student could join. Office bearers had to be elected each year for the union as well as for these associations. While elections for the union secretary's position were hotly contested, for most others, the head of the department or the senior staff member in charge would name a secretary at the first meeting, and soon enough, I was named secretary of the economics society of the college. Involvement in such activities inevitably extended the time I spent away from home and helped enlarge the range of my interests. Additionally, one had to supplement whatever was taught in the classroom with extensive reading outside; more time was devoted each year for library work and group discussions with or without faculty members. Between the union and other student associations, a number of debates and lectures by distinguished visitors were organised every term. In the six years I spent in the university, the visitors included vice-chancellors and eminent professors from other universities, distinguished men of letters, political leaders, editors and artists.

A few years before I completed my graduate course in economics, my father was transferred from Mysore to a small town east of Bangalore. I moved into the college hostel, which was in several ways a new learning experience. However, I missed my family which had given me a sense of belonging and my character. It had given me a feel for austerity, tolerance and the capacity to enjoy simple pleasures. I had developed a ear for music and a taste for Kannada and English literature largely due to my elder brother, who owned a bookshop.

The decades of the 1930s and 1940s contributed to my development in various ways, besides enabling me to complete my academic career. They were indeed momentous decades for the entire world, moving rapidly from the Great Depression of the late 1920s through fascism and Nazism to World War II, from laissez-faire capitalism to Franklin Roosevelt's New Deal, Keynesian economics, full-employment policies and Marxian socialism to Leninism, Stalinism and Maoism, from nuclear fission to Hiroshima and Nagasaki. Great changes had also occurred in the physical, life and social sciences and arts and literature, transport and communications, education and health services. After the enormous destruction of the war years, the world fondly dreamt of quieter times, hoping that the United Nations (UN) and its associate bodies would deliver peace and progress. These hopes were soon rudely shattered in India as elsewhere.

Even before the start of World War II, India's struggle for independence had gathered momentum under Gandhi's leadership. Dominion status was no longer the struggle's objective, especially among the younger leaders of the party. In the 1937 provincial election, popular governments, mostly Congress-dominated, had assumed office and initiated a series of social reforms and development measures, substantially different from what the British had thus far done. Besides land reform and debt relief, support to trade unions, and educational reforms, serious thought was given to structural change through promotion of infrastructure and industrial development. This was a major issue as it had to be harmonised with the Gandhian philosophy of rural transformation through support to farmers and small or cottage industries. Far more important was the clear demonstration that governments led by elected representatives were entirely capable of maintaining law and order and spearheading social progress, contrary to whatever had been dinned into the people's ears by the British. With the outbreak of war in 1939, the popular governments were summarily dismissed and India was like all other British or European colonies, dragged physically and financially into the war. But the couple of years of Congress rule had changed the perspective of the younger generations. Total independence had become not just credible but the indisputable objective of political struggle. We were, of course, too callow to recognise the many undercurrents of communal and caste interests, class conflicts, language or occupational differences and so forth, which were later to crop up and alter the shape of the final outcome. But the dream of a free, fully independent and fast-developing India was too attractive to us just coming out of academia, to worry about other things.

IV

Contrary to my expectations, I found that a good master's degree was not adequate to secure a worthwhile job in the Mysore state or elsewhere. By the time I was out of college, in all of south India as well as Maharashtra, being a brahmin had nearly become a disqualification for government service. I could only secure a minor job at the taluk level. After a year's trial, I decided to quit and try my fortune elsewhere. Around that time, M N Srinivas (who later became an internationally renowned social anthropologist) literally forced me to shift to Bombay University's School of Economics and Sociology (USES). My parents were at first loath to send me but later agreed, though reluctantly. When I set out to Bombay in October 1943, I had no idea what I would do to maintain myself. However, when I registered for my PhD degree at the USES, the director, C N Vakil not only agreed to accept me but gave me a "studentship" of about Rs 30 a month for the rest of the academic year. Besides this immediate relief, he also found me a job in one of the local colleges to teach undergraduate courses in economics and commercial geography. Apparently, my luck had turned. The years I spent as a student in Bombay (1943-47) were in many ways tremendously beneficial. The USES had a fine library with a rich collection of books and journals and I was soon immersed in serious research on questions relating to national income generation and distribution, especially the latter aspect.

My student life in Bombay was very different from that in Mysore. With my earnings I could afford to shift to the university hostel, which was within walking distance of the downtown campus, sharing a room with Srinivas. When I was not lecturing in one of the local colleges, we usually walked down to the school after breakfast and settled down for day-long reading, meeting faculty members and discussing all manner of things with fellow researchers. Each of us had a table in a common room to do our reading and writing. We could borrow books and journals from the library and keep them for as long as we needed. These were all exciting facilities for me and my avidity for study knew no bounds. It was in the USES that I first met I G Patel and B V Krishnamurthi. Their paths and mine were to cross many times in later years.

While studying in Mysore, I had barely touched the fringe of economics. My knowledge was limited to the micro-economics of Alfred Marshall, supplemented a little bit by welfare economics, monetary theory and sundry other issues, including the economic problems of India. It was only after coming to Bombay that I discovered how much economics had advanced in general equilibrium theory, monetary analysis, international trade, economic history and so forth. I got to study Leon Walras, Vilfredo Pareto, Knut Wicksell, Gunnar Myrdal and other European authors, as well as numerous American writers. There were other attendant benefits. Since I had studied mathematics and statistics for my bachelor's course, I could refurbish these disciplines with further reading and discussion with others. I delved deeper into mathematical economics and econometrics and could follow the advances in these areas also. Altogether, the years I spent in Bombay so greatly enriched my knowledge of theoretical economics that I felt bold enough to take up a subject in pure theory for my doctoral dissertation.

The period 1943 to 1947 was also one of historical changes in the country. Just before I went to Bombay, the Indian National

Congress had assembled there and passed the famous "Quit India" resolution. The British government retaliated by arresting all the Congress leaders, including Gandhi. Protest meetings and huge processions took place in the country each day and, inevitably, the police sought to prevent these popular demonstrations. It was impossible to avoid joining the protests, especially after Gandhi began a fast unto death in prison. The university was in turmoil and we could hardly stay indoors. A couple of times, I narrowly missed being arrested and beaten up by the police. It was by then clear that the popular uprising all over the country was unyielding and there could only be one conclusion.

The civil disobedience movement went on without let or laxity until all the leaders were released and the British government started serious negotiations for India's independence in 1944. Bombay's attention then had been diverted by a great fire, which started in one of the cargo ships berthed in the harbour and spread rapidly to the docks, warehouses and surrounding city areas. Life was totally disrupted for almost a month as the fire spread from one area to another and engaged the attention of both the people and the provincial government. But as the fire died down, peoples' resistance resumed. Bombay's labour in textile mills and workshops, public facilities and railways, ship construction and dockworkers, students and teachers all went on a strike. To crown it all, seamen and officers of the Indian navy virtually mutinied. Sardar Patel (who later became India's Home Minister) had to fly down from Delhi and persuade them to wait until the negotiations with the viceroy were complete. But when an agreement was finally reached and India attained freedom from colonial rule in August 1947, the country was partitioned with gruesome consequences which have yet to be remedied.

Several changes had also occurred meanwhile in my personal affairs. Vakil, who had been appointed economic adviser to the newly set up department of planning and development in the Government of India, took me along with him as his research officer, which gave me a first taste of British bureaucratic culture. We were soon back in Bombay, pursuing our usual interests. A little later, I was appointed a lecturer in the USES in a leave vacancy, which among others meant that I had to vacate my room in the university hostel as I ceased to be a student. I moved out to a small hotel on the beach in one of the distant suburbs which was all I could afford on the lecturer's salary. Unfortunately, barely a month later, the hotel caught fire late at night; the boarders rushed out in whatever they were wearing and everything else was burnt down. Apart from my other possessions, I lost the best part of my draft thesis on which I was working that night, a loss which left me desolate. The next morning, I shifted to the apartment of a family friend, who soon equipped me with clothes and other requirements at his expense. With my notes and draft chapters of the thesis irretrievably lost I had to start reconstructing as much of it as I could recollect.

By sheer coincidence, a silver lining appeared on the dark clouds. During my short tenure in the planning and development department, I had been persuaded by Vakil to apply for one of the many scholarships offered by the Government of India for advanced research in the UK and the US. This materialised in the summer of 1947 and admission was secured in the London School of Economics (LSE). I was required by the LSE to inform them of my research subject before joining in September that year. I wrote back saying that I intended to pursue the study on which I was already engaged, "Variation in Relative Shares of Productive Factors in National Income." To my great relief, this was accepted and I spent the couple of months before sailing to London reconstructing the main argument of the draft I had lost in the fire.

Between my return to Bombay from Delhi and my departure for London, two events of life-long importance and pleasure happened. First and foremost, I got married to a second cousin of mine, Madhura, with whose family my father had close relations and whom I had got to know when, as a temporary teacher in the local college, I lived in her father's house for some months. We had thus an opportunity to know each other, though not intimately. The wedding was in May 1947 at her father's place. Within weeks, I had to leave for Bombay to prepare for my voyage to London and we could not really spend much time together. Nor could I take her with me to London as my scholarship was barely adequate for my keep. We thus had no alternative to pursuing our studies separately, thousands of miles away from each other. It was only after my return to India to work for the Planning Commission in Delhi that we could set up house together.

The second event of importance in my life was getting to know Sachin Chaudhuri, a person of extraordinary ability and charm.

Sachin was formally registered in the USES as a doctoral student, but in reality was the general manager of a film-producing company in Bombay. When my friend Srinivas and I first met him, he was in a smart business suit and an expensive tie in a sumptuous office on one of Bombay's busy streets. It was a short meeting over tea and pastries, during which he said that he had some project in mind which he wished to discuss with us and would we be good enough to have dinner with him at his house a few days later? His apartment was fairly close to the university and when we went there, he had with him his younger brother Hiten and a couple of others whom we got to know well later. The project Sachin and his brother had in mind was to start a weekly magazine in which economic, social, political and cultural subjects could be discussed freely, regardless of one's basic philosophy on such matters. Its columns were to be open to all those who had something worthwhile to say on economic development, democracy and social justice, the lessons of history as well as the road to brave new worlds, indeed anything which derived from honest intellectual effort and benefiting essential social values. We could not of course settle all this that evening and it was not until after both Srinivas and I left for England that Sachin resigned his position with the film company and with his brother Hiten embarked on serious preparations for the journal.

The first issue of *The Economic Weekly* (*EW*) with Sachin as editor appeared on 1 January 1949, as "an Independent weekly to deal primarily with economic problems of the country, and then with the broad political ones as they impinge on the former". The purpose was to generate "light without heat", to provide a forum for young social scientists who were trying to take wing. What started then as a modest effort soon attained a position of importance and influence; and the journal's new version, the *Economic and Political Weekly* (*EPW*), has become, thanks to a succession of brilliant and dedicated editors, a publication of high international standing. Starting as its London correspondent in the earlier years, my relationship with it over the decades became very close, with immense benefit to me intellectually and, equally importantly, emotionally.

By the time I left for London many changes had occurred in the family. My father had again been posted in Mysore, and three of my six sisters had been married. The household at that time consisted of my aged grandmother, my parents, my brother Narayana Swamy and his wife, besides my young sisters and an even younger brother Srinivas. My brother's bookshop was some distance away from home but within easy reach of the colleges and high schools. It had also become a meeting place for the local intelligentsia, especially Kannada literati of the younger generation. Narayana Swamy had been deeply engaged in translating Gandhian writings into Kannada. It was in his bookshop that I gathered my literary legacy.

V

I left for London in late August 1947, soon after India's first independence day on a British steamer which had not yet been reconverted to civilian use. Some 90 of us going abroad for higher studies were billeted in a deck house built for transporting troops to theatres of war, with rows of three-tiered bunks and common baths. The cabins on the decks were occupied by British civilian and military officers who were returning home after their India stint. Though we could wander around freely on the decks, we were not altogether welcome in lounges or the main dining hall. The deck-house we occupied was obviously meant for subalterns of the British army who could not mix freely with captains and above or with British members of the Indian Civil Service (ICS). However, the library and sports deck were part of the common space for all passengers. We had sailed during the monsoon, when the Arabian Sea was very rough and wet and it was not until we were in the Suez Canal that deck-sports became possible. But the library which consisted mostly of light reading was open all the time and many of us spent our waking hours there or in the few covered enclosures on the upper decks. We docked in London after about a fortnight and took the special train to St Pancras station where we were received by a couple of India House officials who helped us reach wherever we were housed. I was taken to a hostel for Indian students in Kensington Gardens Square run by the University of London. I lived there until my return to India.

My first week in London was spent on arrangements for living in the hostel for a long time. Virtually everything was in short supply in post-war Britain and strictly rationed. I was advised by the hostel authorities to obtain the essential documents for registration as a student, secure ration books, and open a bank account. With some assistance, I found my way to the Indian High Commissioner's office (India House) for the entitlement to the LSE. Armed with these, I could quickly secure from the ration office the book of "points", which were to be surrendered with each purchase of milk, foodstuff, clothes, chocolates, tobacco and so on. While meat and eggs were rationed, fish, fruits and vegetables were not – but for that reason, tended to be expensive. Likewise, though one could buy lunches and dinners in restaurants, they did not come cheap and could be had only occasionally. The next few days I spent getting to know the local bus and train routes, as well as the shops and eating places in the vicinity.

My first visit to the LSE a week or so later was not an exciting one. Housed in a side street off Aldwych, the LSE did not have the facade of an institution of learning like that of my college in Mysore or of the University of Bombay. It looked more like a workhouse, a habitation for the Fagins and Oliver Twists of London. But this impression did not last long. Once I saw the school's magnificent library, its annex for researchers, the lecture halls, students' common room and above all the eminence of the faculty and the rich variety of students from all parts of the world, I felt reassured that the LSE would help my intellectual development. The LSE had some other benefits. India House, which was literally across the street, had dining room facilities where one could eat Indian lunches and snacks. Many distinguished visitors from India could be met there and the then High Commissioner V K Krishna Menon was for long a friend of the LSE and a frequent visitor there. We were also within reach of the Thames Embankment, St Pauls, the British Museum and other London landmarks, including the theatre world. Very soon, most of my waking hours were spent in the LSE and its environs, where with guidance from my friends, I learnt to live quite fruitfully within my stipend.

Britain's Labour Party had come to power at the end of World War II and had embarked on an ambitious programme of social and economic reform. The LSE then had the reputation of being the British government's think tank, led by Harold Laski, Beveridge, W A Robson and others. It was also host to distinguished liberal economists such as Lionel Robbins, F A Hayek and Peter Bauer, who strongly resisted the Fabian socialism of the Labour government. Fundamentally, the liberal economists were against the macroeconomic management philosophy of the Cambridge school of J M Keynes, Richard Kahn, Nicholas Kaldor, Richard Stone and others, and even more opposed to Marxian economists. Despite the successful application of macro-management techniques to control private expenditure for war financing, Robbins and others apparently hoped for a return to free-market conditions in the post-war years. But this did not happen. The Labour government had embarked on programmes such as the National Health Scheme, a full-employment policy, nationalisation of basic industries and public utilities, and so on. All these involved additional public expenditure, which had to be financed through heavy borrowing domestically as well as abroad besides heavy taxation. Domestic prices, which had been well controlled during the war years, moved up despite rationing and heavy imports, compelling the UK to devalue the pound, limiting the access of countries like India to accumulated sterling balances and seeking US assistance under Marshall Aid. Altogether, it was a time of intense activity and fierce academic debate in which the LSE was heavily involved. For me, as *The Economic Weekly's* London correspondent, there was a plethora of topics to write on, much to my benefit.

The two and a half years I spent in London were not hard, despite the rationing of food and the limited funds at my disposal. At the LSE, I soon got to know British and other students who were well off and could afford to invite me to their homes or take me out for lunches at expensive restaurants, concerts and plays. Most of them, especially the Canadians, Americans and South Africans, lived well and entertained frequently. These were also occasions for them to know more about India, its politics and economics, besides Indian society and culture. Not that I was an expert on any of these, but their knowledge of these matters was limited or deeply influenced by British versions of India, and they were eager to speculate on which way "Independent India" would go. Some of the political students (like Pierre Trudeau, who later become the Canadian Prime Minister) were aware of Prime Minister Nehru's leanings towards socialist programmes, as well as Gandhi's preference for rural reconstruction, and they strongly believed that India was more likely to move towards the Soviet model rather than the US one. These *addas* (informal exchanges) went on for hours, with much consumption of beer, cigarettes and good food.

My colleagues' interest in Indian affairs became much more intense after the assassination of Gandhi in January 1948. Conditions in both India and Pakistan were truly horrendous after Partition and the Gandhi assassination made things very difficult for Nehru's government as well as the refugees and everybody else. In the absence of a properly articulated constitution for the country, those in charge had to "make do" with whatever was at hand. It was not until 1950 that things began to settle down. But the period 1947-1950, which coincided with my London years, were exceedingly difficult ones for India and there was no end to the speculation of my friends on India's future.

London at that time was also host to a large body of Indian students studying in the many colleges there. Many of them had come together to form the Federation of Indian Students' Associations (FEDIND), which was dominated then by the leftists. At the convention of FEDIND during the summer of 1948, at Loch Lomond, I was elected as a secretary, essentially as a compromise candidate, acceptable to both the communists and the rest. I continued in that position until September 1949, when I buckled down to writing my thesis for submission to the board of examiners in early 1950. Since my Government of India scholarship was only for two years, I had to seek an extension of it through India House. However, New Delhi was not prepared to grant it, as it had come to consider FEDIND a communist outfit and I had become persona non grata. It was a dire situation for me until Krishna Menon intervened and secured for me a loan from the government to cover my living expenses for six months. This was barely adequate and I had to supplement it with the fees I got for teachers under the Worker's Education Programme and for my contributions to *The Economic Weekly*. My association with FEDIND continued to interfere with my career in several ways even after my return to India and it took many years for the Home Ministry to fully accept my bona fides.

Returning to India after an absence of almost three years was something of a shock. London was populous but organised; in contrast, Bombay seemed very crowded and confusing. Tickets for train journeys had become difficult to obtain and it was only through the intervention of a senior official of the railway company that I could secure one to go to Bangalore. Even so, I reached a day later than expected, much to the disappointment of my wife and others who had gathered the previous evening at the station. So was I by the delay. When I went home to Mysore with my wife, they were happy to see me but it took some time for us to feel easy with one another. Needless to say, I was greatly relieved to see them in reasonable health and spirits. I was not in a hurry to report to the Government of India, as my wife and I were seeing each other after nearly three years and we could not have enough of each other. I also took time off to see my professor and others in the economics department of the old college.

2

Delhi: The First Planning Commission

I

THE Planning Commission (commission or PC hereafter) had been set up in 1950, soon after President Rajendra Prasad assumed office under India's new Constitution. The presidential order under which it was established required it to prepare plans for India's economic development, bearing in mind the government's constitutional obligations. It was to be an advisory body to the central and state governments, despite the prime minister being its chairman. As a returning government scholar, I was asked to report to the PC's economic division.

It had long been held that much of India's poverty was due to laissez-faire and imperial preference policies pursued by the British in the 19th and 20th centuries. India had been used as a raw material producing colony; apart from the jute, sugar and cotton textile industries, no sizeable metal or manufacturing industries existed. The Indian rupee was linked to the pound sterling and much of trade financing was done by exchange banks headquartered in the UK. The stock exchanges were literally "share bazaars". The need for industrial development had long been desired by Indians and with the Constitution specifically directing that the ownership and control of the material resources of the community should subserve the "common good", it was clear that the state should actively participate in the country's economic activity.

In the years following the Great Depression of 1929, most countries wanted their governments to play a more active role in mitigating the severe ups and downs of capitalist economies. This was particularly evident after the rapid industrial advance of the Soviet Union, President Franklin Delano Roosevelt's New Deal in the US, the growth of socialist parties in Europe and the emergence in the UK of the Keynesian theses of demand management through compensatory budget policies. In this climate, it was natural for India's Congress Party to explore, in the 1930s, the scope for more effective participation by the government of independent India in planning for economic progress. No clear ideas of what form such planning should take or how it could be implemented had, however, emerged. But when Nehru became the Congress president in 1938, initial steps were taken by that party and a national planning committee was appointed under his chairmanship. Despite the start of the war in 1939, the committee continued its work and produced several reports on different aspects of planning and development. However, all this was overshadowed by the party's intensified political struggle until the war ended and India gained independence.

Besides the Congress Party, others had also veered towards planning. The "Bombay Plan" by a group of eminent industrialists, the People's Plan of the M N Roy faction and the Gandhian plan of Sriman Narayan and J C Kumarappa had all envisaged an active economic role for the government in future years. Even the Government of India had set up a planning and development department in 1944. This was short-lived, but before it folded up, it fashioned an industrial policy statement. This statement did not specify the role of government in any detail, but it indicated fairly clearly the need for promoting one way or another a variety of essential industries in the post-war years. None of these plans or policies could be acted on immediately after 1947. The Government of India had yet to establish its executive authority in matters of civil administration and defence, integrate the numerous princely states and settle millions of refugees. The Constituent Assembly set up in December 1946 was still debating the country's political structure, its constituents and its fundamental objectives.

The fully articulated Constitution setting out the main objectives and basic structure of the country's polity was adopted in January 1950. It provided for a union or central government and for several state governments with identified resources and responsibilities and the separation of legislative, executive and judicial responsibilities in all cases. Besides the national parliament and states' legislatures, it also set up the country's Supreme Court, Auditor-General and Election Commission separately. The Constitution's principal objective was to establish a secular, sovereign democratic republic in which social, economic and political justice, equality of status and opportunity, freedom of thought, expression, belief and faith were to be secured for all its citizens. These features of the Constitution were to inform in appropriate ways any and all of the policies or activities that the central and state governments may undertake. When, therefore the PC was set up by the central government in 1950 by a presidential order, these constitutional injunctions and values had to be respected. In its turn, the PC advised all state governments to make arrangements for preparation of development programmes in conformity with these principles.

II

At the time I joined, the PC had started functioning in the south wing of Rashtrapathi Bhavan, with part of its offices in the other wing. Except the prime minister, who was the PC's chairman, the deputy chairman, other members and senior officers had their rooms in the southern wing. When I reported in August 1950 to the chief of the economic division (J J Anjaria), I was asked to share an office with K N Raj, then assistant chief of the division in the same wing. Anjaria and Raj were like me products of the LSE, the former in the 1930s and the latter during the war years. It was in some ways odd that three former students of the LSE, which by then had turned libertarian, should be so fully occupied with planning for a new India.

Besides the prime minister, who usually came to preside over the PC's meetings, each of the members was in charge of a major sector of the economy. Thus, the deputy chairman, G L Nanda, looked after the PC's day-to-day administration besides employment and related problems; V T Krishnamachari, the general administration, co-ordination with other ministries and state governments; C D Deshmukh, finance and foreign exchange; R S Patil, agriculture and the rural sector; and G L Mehta, the industries and energy sectors. While the Cabinet Secretary was ex-officio secretary of the PC, it was the deputy secretary, Tarlok Singh, who really managed its affairs. Belonging to the Indian Civil Services (ICS), Tarlok Singh had very ably handled the resettlement of thousands of refugees from Pakistan in Punjab and elsewhere and earned Nehru's confidence as a dedicated public servant and diligent officer. He was also a trained economist, with special concern for agriculture and development planning (like us in the economic division, he was also a product of LSE).

Apart from Nanda and Deshmukh (who continued to be a member after he assumed charge of the Ministry of Finance) there was no other Cabinet minister in the PC.

At the division chiefs' level, the PC had gathered specialists from wherever they could find them. Thus Anjaria (and Raj) had come from the Reserve Bank of India's (RBI) research department; Y S Pandit of the industries division from the research section of Tata Sons Ltd; and B N Datar of the labour and employment division from the Maharashtra government's statistical office. There was no division for agriculture as the ministry concerned had a strong research department. The small administrative office was headed by K Bharatan, who was already in government service. My wife and I developed close relations with all of them, particularly with Raj and Datar, who shared an apartment. They virtually became family members. We often met in Datar's apartment in the evening with other common friends, for relaxation and some merriment. This group held together for long; and when in late 1954, I went to Delhi on some errand, they all gathered to celebrate the birth of my daughter Bansi.

Delhi of the 1950s was a much safer and less crowded city than now, despite the influx of thousands of refugees from Pakistan. Most of them were still in the process of settling down in massive temporary colonies in Faridabad or other outlying areas. Apart from the barracks built for the army during the war, very little new construction was taking place. Many offices, as well as officers, had been allotted space in these barracks. Like other junior officers of the PC, I was temporarily accommodated in a room in Constitution House, where several members of the Constituent Assembly stayed. However, when my wife joined me some months later, I had to move out. A senior officer who had been allotted a set of rooms in the barracks on Ferozshah Road was kind enough to let us occupy one of the rooms, which for many months was our living room, kitchen, storeroom and all else. When he left New Delhi, we moved into an even smaller room on Raisina Road which, however, was closer to the office and had been specifically allotted to me.

Living conditions in Delhi were not much different from what they were during the war years. Wheat, rice, sugar and kerosene were rationed and generally of poor quality. With massive government purchases to feed the refugee camps in Kurukshetra and elsewhere, price increases could not be stemmed with additional supplies. The loss of Burma as well as large portions of Punjab and Bengal to Pakistan had made the rice and wheat outputs of these regions unavailable to independent India. With the outbreak of the Korean War, food prices had risen sharply in most world markets and imports could not be secured cheaply or in adequate quantity. As a last resort, Nehru sought a wheat loan from the US, which could reach local markets only by 1951-52. In these conditions, controls were reimposed in 1950-51. The foodgrains production index, which in 1950-51 had reached a low of 57 (triennium 1969-70=100), went up gradually to 75 in 1953-54, and together with imports and food controls, helped prevent runaway inflation. It was not until 1958-59 that food prices started rising again, pulling up the wholesale price index and cost of living with them (of this later).

III

When the PC started work on the First Five-Year Plan in 1950-51, it was not writing on a clean slate. Some years earlier, India and Sri Lanka had met in Colombo and drawn up what came to be known later as the Colombo Plan. The idea was, perhaps, that the projects which figured in this plan could draw on sterling balances which had accumulated to their credit during the war. The Colombo Plan for India was a modest one consisting mainly of projects and programmes related to the agricultural sector. The principal objective was to get started, to enable the agricultural sector to enhance the available supplies of food and raw materials as quickly as possible.

Many of these schemes had been started by the time the PC got organised and had therefore to be considered as part of future Plans. This was not entirely a disadvantage, since growing more food was a matter of high priority, both to enhance food supplies and to provide rural employment. The PC also felt that without a substantial increase in the production of food and of the raw materials needed for industry it would be impossible to sustain a higher tempo of development in other sectors. It was recognised that in its formative period, the country's financial and administrative resources could not be overstretched, especially when so little preparatory work for detailed formulation of plans and programmes had been done. Basic factual information on the Indian economy was grossly inadequate. Reliable data on important aspects such as the gross domestic product (GDP), its principal components, savings and investment, imports and exports, financial structure and flows, and so on, were largely unavailable at that time and the organisation necessary for collecting such information was in the process of being set up. The PC had to draw up the First Five-Year Plan on the basis of intelligent guesses for the economy as a whole and confine its planning to the public sector in the centre and states, virtually restricting itself to a five-year budget of outlays on projects and programmes together with a financing scheme.

As far as the central government was concerned, information on its revenue and capital budgets was available in sufficient detail. But it had to be reclassified in accordance with the economic categories of development and non-development outlays for each year and of receipts according to their sources. As for states, while budgetary data for the former provincial governments were similar to those of the centre, information for the princely states, which continued or were merged with neighbouring states, was both inadequate and inadequately articulated. I shall come back to this later.

Some estimates of India's national income had been attempted by economists for specific years from time to time. The last of these was by V K R V Rao for 1931-32 for "British India". This was not comparable to later estimates as it excluded the princely states but included what later became Pakistan. It was essentially an estimate of "originating product" of different sectors of the economy and differed conceptually from the gross (or net) magnitudes derivable from "national income accounts" prepared under the UN around 1950. In the absence of these numbers on the basis of which macro-magnitudes could be projected for five years or longer, the PC had to make a series of plausible assumptions. Thus for the First Plan period, it assumed a population growth of 1.25 per cent per annum, a domestic saving rate of 5 per cent of national income and a capital/output ratio of 3:1 for setting out the long-term perspective, as well as for policy recommendations on such matters as required additional saving and investment, anticipated increase in per capita income and consumption, resource mobilisation and so forth. Recognising the difficulties of detailed planning in the absence of reliable estimates of macro-magnitudes, the PC lent full support to setting up the National Income Unit (NIU) for continuous work on a system of national income accounts for the Indian union as well as the National Sample Survey Organisation (NSSO), both under the guidance of P C Mahalanobis, statistical adviser to the government and director of the Indian Statistical Institute (ISI) in Calcutta. Within the government, data collection had been organised in some ministries for particular items. Besides budgetary details available from the Ministry of Finance, the economic adviser's office in the Department of Commerce collected regular information on wholesale prices, imports and exports, the Department of Agriculture on the area and output of different crops, the Department of Labour on labour statistics and so on. But these were confined to "British India" and derived more from the government's concern for the collection of customs duties, land revenue, price controls and so on rather than a desire to understand the structure of the economy or changes in it. Information on conditions in princely states and private sectors of industry and trade remained scanty until after the country was integrated and specific arrangements made for the regular flow of information to the Central Statistical Organisation (CSO).

All these were later developments. When we started putting together the extant knowledge of the Indian economy, we could not go far. While the UN System of Social Accounts was available, the NIU had yet to provide reliable data on the country's GDP. We had to arrive at tentative estimates of the principal macroeconomic items which seemed plausible. We then tried these out on those in the NIU and other knowledgeable persons, chiefly Rao, who had been involved in such exercises earlier. His estimates were, however, confined to "British India" before Partition and they could not give us (or him) a feel of what independent India's national aggregates could be. Altogether, we could only second-guess the macro-magnitudes and place them before the PC. Without going into much detail, the PC went along with our "guesstimates". But to be on the safe side, it recognised that it could plan only for the public sector and that too mainly for the central government. With the financial system geared mostly to providing working capital to private trade and factories, and the stock market confined to the activities of brokers, private investment was spotty. It was against this background that the Bombay industrialists' plan had desired the bulk of investment for development to come from the government. That apart, with little basic data from the economy as a whole being available, the PC could only "plan" for the public sector.

IV

Before any detailed work on planning could be taken up, the PC took a view on how much should be attempted and for what specific objectives. For reasons mentioned earlier, food and other prices had gone up by 1950, and the Korean War had reinforced the argument for avoiding further pressure on prices. This had generated widespread debate on deficit financing for planned investment. In the early 1940s, Vakil had argued how the growth of money supply during the war years had caused a "falling rupee" – a big rise in prices. Similarly in the 1950s, B R Shenoy put forth forcefully the case against deficit financing. Thus, one of the questions the PC had to tackle was whether, in working out the financing scheme for the Five-Year Plan, the central budget could resort to deficit financing and if so, to what extent.

During the war years, the UK, the US and several other countries, including India, had resorted to deficit financing on a large scale. In each case, different policies had been adopted to counter the possible adverse effects of this budgetary recourse. Budgetary deficits were initially allowed in the US to raise private expenditure, but additional taxation and price regulations were introduced to reduce the inflationary impact of private consumption expenditure as the war progressed. In the UK, which started preparing for the war earlier, policies of demand management, through additional taxation, public borrowing, price controls and rationing, were undertaken, enabling the country to prevent inflationary pressures. These experiences had led many developing countries like India to view deficit financing of development expenditure favourably, provided adequate steps were taken to avoid undue pressure on domestic prices or an adverse impact on balance of payments. The latter was not an immediate worry to the PC, as substantial sterling balances had accrued to India's credit during the war years, and could be drawn upon to supplement domestic supplies. It was also felt that when the agricultural schemes started under the Colombo Plan bore fruit, home supplies would increase and have a salutary effect on prices. All told, the PC had accepted the possibility of utilising budget deficits as a means of financing Plan expenditure. The UK's experience of financing war expenditure had convinced me that deficit financing for development could be possible, provided some offsetting policies such as increased supply of wage goods, additional taxation and rationing were adopted and I was in favour of taking this risk. After some further discussion within the economic division and with the finance minister, we also got the PC to agree. But deficit financing to what extent remained a matter to be decided on the basis of the Plan size and resource mobilisation through additional taxation, government borrowing and so forth.

While the Plan size was to some extent dependent on the forecast of resources likely to be available over the five-year period, what needed to be sought in each sector of the economy and in what manner were matters to be placed before the PC by the members concerned. This was in some ways a chicken and egg problem. What came first – what to include in the Plan or what resources could, in fact, be mobilised? In the PC, there was hardly any difference of opinion on the need for a jump-start in the first five years if the country as a whole were to achieve all-round development. However, the prevailing conditions, apart from the scope for mobilisation of resources, obliged the PC to proceed cautiously.

For one thing, the price situation was such as to lend force to the argument of those who held that budgetary policy should avoid incurring deficits annually to support development outlays, especially on projects with long gestation periods. It was clear even then that without a steady and quick growth in agricultural supplies, it would not be possible to hold the price line. Relief and rehabilitation of refugees was still a heavy burden, financially as well as administratively. Further, the position in states differed widely and it was hard to decide how much planning they could undertake effectively on their own. In both the agricultural and industrial sectors, the sentiment was in favour of the public sector undertaking large development projects, not only because of lack of adequate financing facilities for private investment but also for the benefit of small farmers and industrial labour. On the external front, the scope for aid in one form or another was very limited as the World Bank as well as the US and the USSR were deeply involved in the reconstruction of war-damaged economies in

Europe and elsewhere. It was also not easy to utilise sterling balances freely because the UK maintained that this amounted to "unrequited exports".

Considering all this, the PC decided to take a view first on its existing budgetary commitments and then consider what further steps could be taken for additional taxation as well as deficit financing. As for taxation, though some of the levies had been raised during the war years, the PC was anxious to avoid a big increase in indirect tax, which would affect prices adversely. On grounds of equity and progressivity, the PC preferred levying income and corporation taxes, as also wealth taxes for additional resources. But at the existing level of industrial activity and non-agricultural incomes, the scope for higher direct taxes was limited. The political position of most parties was against continuation of land revenue or other imposts on the agricultural sector; they favoured abolition of *zamindari* in all the states. Altogether, the PC had to relate additional levies to the new incomes to be generated during the Plan period, keeping in view the constitutional obligation to seek a reduction of inequalities in income and wealth. Besides all this, the many schemes started earlier under the Colombo Plan, especially in the agricultural sector, had to be completed and other committed revenue expenditures fully provided before undertaking additional spending.

This budgetary analysis was the responsibility of the economic division and Raj and I were asked to look into these questions and come up as early as possible with plausible estimates of financial resources likely to be available for Plan expenditure. This was more easily said than done, as the budget details conformed to accounting classifications devised for seeking parliamentary approval by each ministry. These had to be reorganised to derive the categories of income, consumption, saving and investment required by the PC and then projected for succeeding years. While initiating this task in association with the Ministry of Finance, we also sought details of the NIU's estimates of macro-magnitudes conforming to the UN system of National Accounts. The NIU's first estimates for 1950-51 were in the process of being developed and they could offer us only "guesstimates" based on partial data. However, since we had yet to complete our budgetary analysis, we decided to come back to national income projections later, after the NIU could offer a firmer basis.

The format for budgetary analysis we subsequently worked out in consultation with Finance Ministry officials was based on separating non-Plan (non-development) outlays to be incurred on existing commitments of one kind or another from both the revenue and capital expenditures. These included, among others, civil administration and defence, contractual payment obligations and recurrent or non-recurrent relief expenditures which did not add to the community's productive capacity. Matching these against revenues from taxes and fees, profits of public enterprises (for example, the railways and posts and telegraphs) and other casual receipts, we assessed the balance available for Plan expenditure from current revenue at present taxes. For later years, we had to add revenues from additional taxes levied from year to year and project all this for the Plan period on the basis of anticipated annual increases in national income. On the government's capital accounts, we took note of their net borrowing and grants from domestic or foreign sources. The extent of deficit financing in the Plan period was derived by setting the aggregate of revenue and capital collections against the proposed Plan outlay. However, to ensure that there was no pressure on prices, we suggested that the overall budgetary deficit should be limited as far as possible to the import surplus available each year. (The PC continues to work with this format even today, with very minor changes. However, the debate on deficit financing continues unabated.)

V

At the PC level, the main debate was on the priorities to be emphasised in the Plan. This required decisions on both the objectives of resource use as well as its pattern. Part IV of the Constitution had laid down in some detail the directive principles of state policy, which required it to promote the welfare of the people by "securing and promoting as effectively as it may be a social order in which justice, social, economic and political, shall inform all the institutions of the national life" (Article 38 [1]). The PC clearly was among the institutions to be so "informed" and the initial discussions were about what this implied. What exactly was meant by "economic justice"? If this had to be secured for people in general, what were the best means to be followed? Since the majority of Indians lived in rural areas, should their interest be safeguarded before other tasks were taken up? While poverty alleviation was a desideratum, should this be related to more employment or increased productivity or both? What about structural modifications, which were likely to contribute to both long-term growth and economic independence? A myriad of such questions kept cropping up each time the PC deliberated on its responsibility as an adviser to central and state governments.

On these questions, the PC members held varying positions with greater or less conviction. Prime Minister Nehru had strong views on which way the economy should go and the government's high responsibility to take the country along that road. He had no doubt that in many areas it was the duty of the state to occupy the "commanding heights", so that the benefits of development could be more evenly distributed. While this was not much disputed in the case of major industries, transport and communications, both Nanda, the deputy chairman, and Patil, the member for agriculture, held that this could not be extended to agriculture, small industries and so forth in the rural sector, as had been done in the USSR. Nehru also did not favour collectivisation of farming operations, nationalisation of trade and the like. He accepted that what the country needed was growth in a "mixed economy" of public and private enterprise; what he had in view was essentially state sponsorship of basic and capital goods industries, which needed large investments and modern technology.

This, in turn, generated a long discussion on patterns of industrialisation which would be beneficial to both output growth and greater employment. There were at that time a number of economists who held that the country's large surplus of labour was a real resource available for development and should be effectively utilised by adopting "labour-using" rather than "capital-intensive" technologies. Also, following the Gandhian philosophy of "self-sufficient village economies", some of the leading political figures disfavoured labour-saving technologies, which could encourage centripetal forces in economic life and thereby in political affairs. This was a view forcefully presented by J C Kumarappa when he met the PC. It was also the position of President Rajendra Prasad and several others in the Congress Party. On grounds of employment of a good proportion of rural labour, small-scale and cottage industries had to be accorded a place in the Five-Year Plans, a proposition which the PC recognised.

Nehru agreed that some form of protection to small-scale and cottage industries was necessary in the short period, but he was very firm that it could not be the basis for long-term growth of the economy, or for technological progress. Both these required the creation within the economy of a capacity to produce industrial machinery of all types together with the raw materials needed by them. Nehru also believed that it was necessary to shift surplus labour away from agriculture to facilitate an increase in agricultural productivity and adopt technological innovations that would help this. In his view, it was time that India developed a flourishing sector of manufacturing industries, as the USSR and Japan had done more recently and as the UK, the US and other countries of the developed world had achieved in earlier centuries. He visualised a long-term perspective of growth involving major reform of land systems, higher yields from land and transfer of labour to non-farm occupations; a change in India's economic structure through extensive industrialisation; more facilities for education, health and other social services; and a doubling of per capita income in the foreseeable future. He observed that people expected his government to take the lead in development processes and was confident of securing all support from them.

While the other members saw the need for a structural change in India's economy, they did not fully share his confidence that the state could take on this responsibility in the First Five-Year Plan. For one thing, Mehta, the PC member in charge of industry, felt that the private sector's role in industrial development should not be downplayed and that incentives should be provided to it. For another, Finance Minister Deshmukh was not sure that the mobilisable resources for the Plan could accommodate a large investment in industries, given the many commitments that the government had already undertaken. Altogether, the PC felt that these matters required closer scrutiny and remitted them to the chiefs of the economic and industries divisions for further study.

As the economic division perceived it, the basic question was how much could the economy as a whole invest in the Plan period without generating inflationary pressures? This depended on ensuring, on the one hand, an adequate supply of food and other essential commodities or services (or wage goods) and, on the other, just enough consumption and investment expenditures to absorb these supplies. As investment in the system depended mostly on available domestic savings, there was also the related problem of estimating the flow of future savings, income and consumption. The NIU could provide only some indication of what they could be, on the scattered information that was available to it. The RBI's published data relating to time deposits, balance sheets of corporate enterprises, insurance and provident fund collections and so on, provided some idea of financial savings in the economy and corporate investments. But on real capital formation, stocks and the like, we drew a blank and had to fall back on plausible guesses. Altogether, the best guess that we could make at that juncture was that domestic savings could not be more than 5 per cent to 7 per cent of national income, estimates which were obviously subject to errors of an unknown magnitude. This was not a level of savings which would permit the aggregate investment required for all-round development of the kind the country required or the PC desired. As we saw it, aggregate savings could go up only if society saved increasingly higher proportions of additional incomes as they accrued from year to year. How much more should be so saved and by what means became matters which the PC had to deliberate on along with a clearer definition of priorities in investment and the respective roles of the central and state governments as also the private sector.

Since the Constitution had laid down that the state should "within the limits of its economic capacity and development, make effective provision for securing the right to work, to education and to public assistance in cases of unemployment, old age, sickness and disablement and in other cases of undeserved want" (Article 41), the PC had to provide in the Plan for public expenditure on health and education among other services. Given the millions who had no means to have their children educated or ensure the health of their family members, it was clear that education and health facilities needed to be expanded significantly and adequate provision made in the Plan for these outlays. These were areas in which Nehru was particularly keen to move fast in rural areas, which badly needed schools and health centres. While recognising that this was primarily the responsibility of state governments, he wanted the central government to give them whatever help it could. In addition, he was anxious that the country should get started on providing facilities for advanced training and research in science and technology. The divisions concerned were asked to work out details of what type of assistance may be needed by state governments for their education and health plans.

VI

For Raj and me, New Delhi in the 1950s was stimulating, challenging and disturbing all at once. Within the PC, we often felt as if we were part of a debating society, where persons of enormous power and responsibility discussed issues of "political economy", technological and social change, economic possibilities and limitations – indeed a myriad of topics of both practical and intellectual import. Underlying all these were fundamental differences in approach among PC members, Cabinet ministers, bureaucrats and academics called in to advise the government and so on. Likewise, different ideas and ideologies dominated social groups, political parties or economic sectors. There was an equally bewildering spread among states, regions or professions. All these factions had their separate visions of what "Independent India" should become. While Raj and I held that India should aim at rapid growth of the industrial sector, Anjaria preferred to focus on agricultural development first. There were Cabinet ministers who were Gandhians, others who wanted India to follow the US model and yet others who preferred the Soviet pattern. Most of the bureaucrats in Delhi tended to adjust their views to those of their ministers, concentrating principally on the sectors under their charge. They admired, in their own way, both the US and the USSR and wished India to emulate them, not blindly but selectively. There were also some, who like President Rajendra Prasad, attached great value to India's spiritual heritage and wished for a modernised, democratic version of some "golden age" of yore. And there were many who wanted changes to happen quickly while others believed that, whatever will be will be, according to the country's karma.

Nehru undoubtedly dominated the scene. It was a period of intense activity, when he literally drove everybody – the government, his party, the PC and so on. In all this he had the tremendous support of the people, despite the hardships of the post-independence years. His "socialistic" leanings were known and to a large extent accepted by most people as necessary to speed up development without exacerbating income and wealth inequalities. He believed equally strongly that these objectives should be so achieved as to strengthen India's federal democracy. This was probably why he wanted the PC to be an advisory rather than an authoritative body, so that its recommendations could be screened to ensure the preservation of most if not all of the citizens' rights enshrined in the Constitution.

The PC did not consist entirely of party members. Three of its six members, Krishnamachari, Deshmukh and Mehta, were persons with an intimate knowledge of administration, finance and corporate industry. Two of the principal advisers to the Prime Minister, Mahalanobis and Gyan Chand, were academics with, if anything, socialist leanings. All division chiefs had different views on the Plan which they expressed freely. Accepting the need for the state's leading role, Krishnamachari stressed administrative concerns, Deshmukh financial limitations and Mehta more space for the private sector. The advisers and officials also had a free say. Nehru took all this in; but in the final decision he had his way, mostly if not fully.

Most of the staff officers were required to attend the PC's meetings and occasionally called upon for their opinion. Since virtually every issue placed before the PC had an economic or financial angle, Anjaria and Raj were often asked for their views. There were also a few occasions for my intervention. In all of these deliberations, questions of both principle and feasibility were dealt with, crisply and seriously. Occasionally, Nehru's impatience showed through if some member or officer went into too much detail or strayed too far out. On such occasions, he was more forthright with his colleagues on the PC than with other officers. Before long, we discovered that when he took out his cigarette holder and cigarettes, he was about to pounce on somebody. But he generally followed this up with something humorous and kind to the person concerned. Among the members, Krishnamachari and Deshmukh had their say quickly, if somewhat ponderously. The others, especially Nanda, tended to be long-winded, which provoked the chairman to say, "Come to the point, I can't sit here all day". But his interest in planning for the welfare of the people was such that he often spent all day, making sure that every aspect of a proposition was closely examined before becoming a part of the programme.

It was necessary to bring together the work of various divisions before papers could be put up for the PC's consideration. Much of this co-ordination was done by Tarlok Singh, the deputy secretary. He was meticulous in his work, polite in his dealings with others and very, very hardworking. His personal staff obviously had a tough time, as he often spent long hours in his office or at meetings of one kind or another. He was quite aware that members of other divisions could not stay all evening, helping him "understand" everything. But he never gave up and did not hesitate to come back to his quest for details, even in PC meetings, until the chairman or one of the members changed the topic. All this notwithstanding, Tarlok Singh effectively brought home to us that we had to make sure of all the details implied in executing the projects and programmes in the Plan. After having spent many years in academic pursuit of abstruse questions of economic analysis, the year or more I spent with the PC helped me appreciate the need for quantification and executability of logically valid propositions. When, in January 1952, I moved to the RBI in Bombay, my strengths and limitations were much clearer to me than earlier.

In the later half of 1951, the RBI had advertised for positions in its research departments. About the same time, Rao, then director of the Delhi School of Economics renewed his offer (which he had made while I was at the LSE) of a lectureship in his institute. I could not accept the latter because of my contract with the Government of India. But my colleagues in the PC suggested I could apply to the RBI on the grounds that it was owned by the Government of India and my working there should be permissible. I sent in my application; after the usual selection process, I was offered the position of senior research officer, with the proviso that I join as soon as I obtained the government's permission. This came in January 1952, after which I left for Bombay.

The 18 months or so I was with the PC greatly clarified my understanding of several aspects of development planning, especially under government auspices. Importantly, in advising the central government, the PC had to evaluate the available choices not merely in terms of economic costs and benefits but from the viewpoint of their political and social suitability. The situation was one in which what looked desirable from one angle was often unfeasible on other grounds. Independence had generated new expectations and new enthusiasms among the people; but the PC had to avoid raising hopes which could not be quickly or fully satisfied, given administrative and other limitations. There was also the need to more clearly assess the economy's strengths and weaknesses at the juncture. The government, in reality, was neither fully organised nor adequately informed of the contours of our economy. Attempts had only just started for systematic collection of qualitative and quantitative information on resources, institutional capabilities, technological conditions, standards of living and so forth by the various ministries in Delhi. This became obvious during the many discussions that Raj and I had with officials in these ministries – most of whom were able, and anxious to take the country forward. All in all, those months made me realise how little I knew about India's economy, its political and social institutions and, above all, its people. It was a sobering experience.

3

With the Reserve Bank of India

I

IN some ways, returning to Bombay after years in London and New Delhi was like a homecoming. My thoughts went back to the excitement of learning new things, gathering experiences outside academia, making new friends and savouring foods the city had to offer. Many of my old friends had stayed on in the Bombay University and elsewhere, and meeting them was an unalloyed pleasure. It was a city whose streets, edifices and transport systems I was familiar with, a city which still had not become a megalopolis. Like in earlier years, it had remained a centre of trade, finance and industry – a gateway not only to India but also the Indian economy. During the years I was away, the *EW* had started on its long journey with Sachin running its editorial affairs in his distinctly original way.

Soon after joining the Reserve Bank (the RBI or the Bank hereafter), I moved into a small hotel in Colaba, which was close to the Bank's central office. The office was an impressive structure, near the Town Hall, India Government Mint, Ballard Estate and the Bombay stock exchange – literally in the centre of the city's business district. The Bank's research department was still small enough for its junior officers to meet and get known to its principal officers – the governor and deputy governors, chief accountant, economic adviser and other heads of departments. As was the usual practice, I was formally introduced by the economic adviser to the governor and deputy governors. Later, I went around on my own to meet the others before settling down to work.

I shared an office with two colleagues on the second floor, with a large window overlooking the harbour. The Bank had an excellent library, lunch rooms and medical assistance in the building. Technically, each of us was part of a division, focusing on particular aspects of monetary and banking policy. It was a different environment, more business-like and better organised than

New Delhi was in those days. As everywhere, housing and essential supplies were in short supply, the building boom was years ahead and Maharashtra had a rigid rent control system which was effectively enforced. Before long, my days fell into a routine of office from ten in the morning to six in the evening, and on most days, evenings with Sachin in the *EW*'s cosy office.

My wife was due to join me after a few weeks and I started looking around for suitable accommodation for the two of us. Though the Bank had some quarters of its own, there were many other officials ahead of me in the queue and I had perforce to look elsewhere. Knowing my plight, Sachin asked us to stay with him while we searched for an apartment. He lived in an old building (Churchill Chambers) very close to the Taj Mahal Hotel, and had an all-purpose man servant, who was nearly as eccentric as Sachin himself, with strong likes and dislikes of his own. It took him and us a little time to get used to each other; very soon, he accepted us completely, thanks largely to my wife's kind treatment. However, life with Sachin was not easy. His lifestyle was totally different from ours and I do not believe we really got used to it as long as we lived there. Some months later, a research officer who had been allotted quarters in one of the Bank's buildings had to go abroad on deputation and I was allowed to occupy it temporarily. Since this was a transitory arrangement, our search for a house continued, though with less urgency.

Before moving out of Churchill Chambers, my wife had been persuaded by a nephew of hers to participate in a Kannada play which Bombay's Mysore Association was to present later in the year. It was the first time a woman was appearing as a leading lady on the association's stage and was thus a special occasion. Since the association was located several kilometres to the north of our lodgings in Colaba, we rode all the way by bus or tram for the rehearsals, traversing markets and masjids, textile mills and temples, hospitals and workers' *chawls* (colonies). After the rehearsals and dinner, we were usually sent back to Colaba by the association's president in his car. The play was a big success, her performance earning much praise and setting the stage for other women joining the drama group. However, it cost us dearly another way. Soon after all this, my wife came down with a severe attack of typhoid, which nearly ended tragically. She took several months to fully recover, by which time my tenure in the Bank's flat was over. She stayed back in her father's home until I could lease a flat of our own in the northern suburb of Khar, through the good offices of an elderly relation of ours, M R Varadarajan of Hindustan Construction Company, a major construction concern in Bombay.

The few months we stayed with Sachin had drawn me further into the *EW*'s affairs. Morning and late evening sessions with him led to wide-ranging discussions on issues in economic policy, social problems and political developments in India or elsewhere; of upcoming social scientists who could provide short or long articles to the weekly; of the principal values of democracy that merit media support and so forth. There were also visitors from different walks of life, both Indian and foreign. Sachin's familiarity with art and literature contributed in a measure to widening our interests in these areas. However, Sachin had no ear for music – an area of special interest to my wife – which surprised us. The months we lived with him not only cemented our friendship and my involvement with the *EW* but was also an enriching experience for both of us.

After bank hours, I stopped often at the *EW*'s office, on the way back to Churchgate. This soon became a routine. Sachin often wanted to pick my brain on matters which he planned to include in the next issue. Discussions often led to my drafting short notes or editorials, often reflecting my views more than Sachin's. But all this was after we had discussed and agreed on who should do what. As always, the editorials or short notes had no names attached to them; but Sachin took full responsibility for them. It was not an easy routine, but being young I could do it for a couple of days each week. It was moreover, creative work untrammelled by other obligations and therefore enjoyable. After I left Bombay, others from the Bank's research departments stepped in to keep the weekly going.

II

Being the central bank of the country as well as its monetary authority, the Bank's principal concerns were financial management and banking regulation. Though banking institutions in India had largely followed the British practice of providing working capital to private trade and industry, the RBI had been required under its Nationalisation Act to also cater to the credit requirements of agriculture and rural industries. With the government assuming developmental responsibilities and foreign exchange management, the Bank's macroeconomic concerns had widened to include price inflation as well as balance of payments.

In the early 1950s, the RBI's department of statistics had embarked on a massive All-India Rural Credit Survey, the collection of corporate balance-sheet data, exchange control statistics and periodic processing of scheduled bank statistics – all of which were to later provide the basis for systematic analysis of the country's monetary and balance of payments positions. Most of these studies were in a rudimentary stage when I joined and there was much exchange of views between economists and statisticians on the measurability of economic concepts, methodology of surveys and operational limitations of data in developing causal connections.

One of my initial assignments was to look closely at the ongoing discussion of deficit financing for development plans, in terms of its relevance to monetary policy. As mentioned earlier, the PC had sought to treat budget deficits as a permissible source of Plan finance under certain conditions, mainly with an import surplus based on a drawdown of sterling balances. As the custodian of the country's foreign assets, the RBI was not particularly keen on such a drawdown, since it meant a substitution of rupee securities for sterling sold to the government. The questions which the Bank's management wanted the research department to explore were how exactly a deficit budget affected the several responsibilities it had assumed as the monetary authority, and what steps it could take to minimise any adverse consequences that may ensue.

The PC had taken the view that additional domestic spending can be prevented from affecting prices by enlarging domestic supplies of essential goods. However, the processes involved in this set-off as well as possible time-lags had not been closely examined by it. These were matters of special concern to the Bank, since it did not want to be blamed for any inflationary consequences. On this detailed exploration of likely effects of budget deficits on money supply and related aspects, my colleague V K Ramaswami (Ramu) joined me and we were able to produce a substantive paper in about three weeks.

The PC's position was that as long as budget deficits were offset by an equivalent sale of foreign balances, there was unlikely to be a sustained increase in money supply. It had also assumed that the release of foreign exchange would add to aggregate supplies on the domestic market. The RBI's concerns were, however, because fiscal deficits added to "reserve money" in the system, on the basis of which additional monetary creation through the banking system could occur. When exactly and how much of this addition to money supply was likely to occur and what steps, if any, should be undertaken to counteract this were moot issues. In the absence of comprehensive data on the aggregate of domestic expenditure in the economy, no reliable money multiplier ratio was available at the juncture. We therefore could present general guidelines in our paper on how successive budget deficits could affect both currency in circulation and scheduled banks' deposits over a period; also when and what sequence of steps by the Bank would be appropriate. However, we could only provide some quantitative examples in support of our suggestions. We also stressed the point that the crucial issue in all this was the assurance of an adequate flow of foodgrains and other wage goods. A good part of Plan expenditure was likely to accrue as income to those with a high propensity to consume and the time profile of increases in consumer spending could not be worked out clearly. In essence, our position was that deficit financing of Plan outlays was not something to be avoided, as long as the government and the Bank were prepared to take effective anti-inflationary measures whenever necessary. Ramu and I were pleased to learn later that the paper was well received within the Bank as well as in New Delhi.

In the subsequent weeks, Ramu and I had a series of discussions with other departmental heads on some of the measures which we thought the Bank could take, on questions of timing as well as feasibility. We also met the governor and deputy governors when they sought clarifications on some of these suggestions. Following internal discussions, we prepared a final version of the document for transmission by the economic adviser to the PC and the Ministry of Finance in Delhi.

When Ramu and I met one of the deputy governors, K Sundaresan, he asked me to stay back after the discussion. As Ramu left, he asked me bluntly if I was a member of the Communist Party of India (CPI). I was taken aback and said "No sir". But as he continued to look sternly at me I then went on to say, "Sir, I have much sympathy for 'socialism', like our prime minister, which is not the creed of the CPI." He said, "Not much difference, is there? Don't both believe in enforcing distributive policies and state dominance?" I replied "Yes sir, that is correct. But I believe socialism is fully compatible with a democratic polity while communism leans towards one-party rule and total centralisation of authority". He seemed satisfied and then asked why the Government of India thought I was a communist. When I told him about the confusion caused by my being secretary of FEDIND in London, he laughed and said he would deal with the Government of India and asked me to forget it. He was thereafter very protective towards me.

The Bank was required under its Act to submit an annual report on its functioning to the Ministry of Finance. Before submitting it to the government, it had to be approved by the central committee of the Bank, consisting of prominent representatives of commerce and industry, agriculture and eminent economists. By the time Ramu and I completed our study of deficit financing, it was time for the research department to start drafting the annual report for 1951-52, due for submission to the government before 30 August 1952. During departmental discussions on the report, the economic adviser sought suggestions on how it could go beyond a summary of the Bank's statement of accounts and activities of its different departments. As newcomers to the Bank, Ramu and I thought we could modify the report and make it an assessment of the economic situation from the RBI's viewpoint. After some discussion, I was asked by the economic adviser to quickly prepare a brief outline of the theme or themes that could be so presented.

The Bank had indeed a good story to tell on developments during the year. Realising that the budget deficits envisaged for financing the First Five-Year Plan could significantly affect both money circulation and inflationary expectations, it had adopted several steps such as raising the Bank rate, restraining its open market operations and starting a bill market scheme to accommodate seasonal variations in trade finance during the year. It was possible to link each of these to subsequent changes in commercial bank lending, their investment in government securities, variations in (narrow) money supply, and price trends in the commodity and securities markets in terms of macroeconomic relationships. In the early 1950s, the Bank's views on monetary and banking matters commanded much respect in the Finance Ministry and government generally. The Government of India had come to depend significantly on the Bank's research department for data and advice on economic trends. Keeping this in mind, I prepared a brief outline of the form the Bank's report to the government could take. When I gave it to the economic adviser, P S Narayana Prasad, he said he would have to check with the governor and let me know. The governor was not averse to the idea of treating the annual report as an occasion for presenting the Bank's views on the developing economic situation and I was asked to go ahead and produce a draft. I was pleased that the governor agreed to this change in the style of its report to the government.

Ramu meanwhile had got busy with trade and payments statistics which the statistics department was trying to systematise. I focused on the monetary and banking developments during the year, discussing issues with my colleagues in the monetary division as well as with those engaged on putting together available data on national income and expenditure. Principally, the report was to be based on a quick analysis of macroeconomic demand and supply and linking these with monetary variations, prices and balance of payments as well as the broad dimensions of the First Plan. As mentioned earlier, the Plan was an extension of commitments already included in the Colombo Plan plus some ex ante investments proposed for the industrial and social sectors. Since all this was before the Imperial Bank of India (which continued to dominate the banking sector) was converted into the State Bank of India, considerable attention had to be paid to the reaction of commercial banks to the Bank's monetary adjustments. These later included changes in the Bank rate, the Bank's willingness to refinance commercial banks and policy directives issued to them from time to time. While it was easy to put together whatever action the Bank took with a view to avoiding undue pressure on prices or exchange reserves, it was not always easy to predict commercial banks' responses to directives issued by the Bank. Altogether, my draft of the report laid out the general argument, leaving room for specific measures taken in response to changes in banks' portfolios to be added by the departments concerned. These details were sent separately by each department to the economic adviser, who passed them on to me with instructions to put them all together in a revised draft to be discussed initially within the research department.

Knowing that the Bank's management was not like the Ministry of Finance in New Delhi, which was very supportive of financing Plan expenditures through budget deficits, it was necessary that the annual report avoided calling attention to later price increases. When I was part of the PC's economic division, I had argued along with Raj that possible price effects could be avoided if the deficits each year were offset by an equivalent drawdown of exchange reserves. This was not something that many in the Bank were happy about, especially because the British government wished to limit these releases each year and the International Monetary Fund (IMF) was in principle opposed to unbalanced fiscal conditions. Prasad, the economic adviser, therefore was asked to make sure the draft represented the Bank's view as precisely as possible. My colleagues in the research department were very supportive of me in traversing this narrow path; most of them took the position that the Bank, in its capacity as adviser to the government, would be justified in taking the position that the financial sector could assist development through limited additions to money supply. If the government thereafter found it necessary to prevent price rises, it should be prepared to take the necessary non-monetary measures and not require the Bank to alter its policy directives to commercial banks.

To cut a long story short, the Bank's report for 1951-52 presented its assessment of the overall economic situation and the extent to which monetary policies could be adjusted in support of development finance, provided the government was prepared to take other control or supply-side measures to allay price rises or price-rise expectations. In due course, the governor informed the economic adviser that the Bank's views on the economic situation and prospects had been well received by the government and commended the research department for giving the annual report a new character. As I had initiated this, it helped add to my prestige as also that of the department within the Bank as well as in New Delhi.

While my wife was recouping from her typhoid attack, I was deputed by the Bank to the Indian Economic Association's annual conference in Trivandrum. I looked forward to meeting Raj there since he was attending the conference from the PC. On the way, I met Alice and Daniel Thorner from the US, who were attending the same session. They were in India to study its agricultural sector, each from a different angle. That was the beginning of a long and fruitful relationship. Due to Daniel's leftist sympathies, he had been asked to appear before the infamous Senator Joseph McCarthy's committee, which he refused. As a result, they had to stay on in Bombay until 1960, after which they shifted to Paris, to the Ecole Pratique des Hautes Etudes of Sorbonne University. They remained in Paris for the rest of their lives, visiting India often and playing host to many Indians in the French capital.

III

Besides fitting the Bank's activities into the macroeconomic framework which the PC was to present shortly as the First Five-Year Plan, my work for the 1951-52 annual report had two direct consequences. In the early part of 1953, the Government of India was to present its report for 1952 to an intergovernmental committee on the Colombo Plan. My former chief in the PC, Anjaria, had by then become economic adviser to the Ministry of Finance, which had the task of preparing the report*. He requested the Bank to lend the ministry my services for a month or so to prepare the draft. Had Raj stayed on in the PC, I would not have had to go to Delhi for this. But by then, Raj had left the government and joined the Delhi School of Economics and I G Patel continued in the IMF. This deputation suited me as my wife was still recuperating in Bangalore after her typhoid attack and the flat I had leased in Khar was not fully ready. After preparing the draft report on the lines suggested by Anjaria in a little over a month, I returned to the Bank in time to shift to our own apartment in Khar.

Later that year, my second task arose as a result of some of the Bank's comments on Plan expectations regarding industrial investment by the private sector. The First Plan envisaged total domestic resources needed for investment by the private industrial sector at Rs 513 crore over its five-year period. In its annual report, the Bank had observed that private investment expenditure was at a low ebb and wondered if the five-year target could be achieved. Some of the leading industrialists also doubted the possibility of

* At that stage, Anjaria was advising both the Finance Ministry and PC. This was not, in my view, a good arrangement, as the bias of the two institutions differed substantially. This continued until 1964, when I became the PC's economic adviser.

high investment in capital goods industries. Besides, the Industries (Development and Regulation) Act of 1951, which stipulated the domains of new investment by the public and private sectors and the continuation of Capital Issues (Control) Act (1943), tended to inhibit private incentives to invest. Bearing these in mind, the government requested the RBI to set up a committee to examine how bank finance on a larger scale could be made available for both fixed and working capital purposes to the private sector. This committee, called the Committee of Finance for the Private Sector, was set up by the Bank in October 1953 under the chairmanship of A D Shroff, a director of Tata Sons Ltd, and consisted of representatives of the major commercial banks, eminent industrialists, the Industrial Finance Corporation of India (IFCI) and an executive director of the RBI. A senior officer from the Bank's department of banking development and I were appointed joint secretaries of the committee, which was required to submit its report to the Bank in about six months.

The Shroff Committee submitted its report in April 1954 to the Bank and through it to the government in New Delhi. In the six months of its existence, I was fully engaged by it and had no other tasks assigned to me by the Bank. To collect information on the working and prospects of the private, non-agricultural sector, the committee travelled all over India meeting industrial interests, banks and other financial institutions, stock market operators, insurance companies and so forth, besides the PC and central and state government ministries. These discussions and the memoranda submitted by various individuals and associations helped me to recognise among other things how government policies intended to achieve certain objectives often evoked private responses of a different kind for reasons which could not be dismissed off-hand. There were also variations of some significance in industrial and business practices from region to region and between large- and small-scale industries. More importantly, it made me see more clearly how lopsided India's industrial development had been, with most of it confined to industries processing agricultural raw materials or fabricating small tools and implements. On the banking side, the main activity was provision of working capital to trade and large-scale industries with agricultural and small-business finance being a virtual monopoly of private moneylenders and traders. Apart from the government-owned IFCI and state finance corporations (SFCs), there were no specialised institutions to support long-term industrial investment by the private sector. The market for new capital issues was very limited and dominated by the textile industries, with Tata's steel industry being a rare exception. Altogether, what soon became clear to the Shroff Committee (and to me) was that the private industrial sector would not be able to meet the investment or production targets envisaged in the First Five-Year Plan without massive financial support from domestic or foreign institutions.

The committee's final recommendations consisted, on the one hand, of modification in the instruments and operations of the RBI, commercial banks, the IFCI and SFCs, and in some of the government regulations affecting market transactions; and, on the other, of the need for specialised "development banks" for enabling newly established companies secure equity as well as long-term loans. These special institutions were to be sponsored by leading banks and insurance companies with RBI and government assistance and support from the World Bank. Not all the committee's recommendations were accepted for reasons of incompatibility with prevailing development and banking policies. Also, at about the same time, the report of the Bank's Rural Credit Survey had become available and the Bank (as well as the Government of India) was focused on enlarging the flow of institutional credit to the agricultural sector. Principally, the government's policy of occupying the economy's "commanding heights" led to the takeover of the Imperial Bank of India, together with a number of commercial banks which had been sponsored by some of the state governments. The Imperial Bank was taken over by the RBI and renamed State Bank of India in July 1955; and those sponsored by state governments were in turn taken over by the State Bank of India in the next few years and constituted as its "associate" banks.

Coming back to the Shroff Committee, two of its recommendations on setting up special institutions were implemented by establishing the Industrial Credit and Investment Corporation of India (ICICI) in the private sector (1954) and the Refinance Corporation for Industry (RCI) in 1956. The former's equity was provided by banks and insurance companies, assisted by the World Bank. The government provided the ICICI with an interest-free loan for several years. As for the RCI, it was wholly owned by the RBI, and was provided access to the US PL-480 counterpart funds, which had by then accumulated to a sizeable amount. The wheat loan from the US had been sold for rupees in India and the proceeds had accumulated to the credit of the US government. It was only later that the US government agreed to re-lend part of these funds to India. However, by late 1954, I had moved over to the rural economics division of the research department and lost track of the committee's other recommendations. Rural economics was a wholly new area for me and after getting to know a bit about India's private industrial sector, I had a chance to learn a little about its agricultural situation. However, before I could settle down in the new division, several things happened.

My wife who had gone to her father's house during the later months of her pregnancy gave birth to a baby girl whom we named Banashankari (which has since been shortened to Bansi). Meanwhile, I had to go to Delhi for an interview with the Union Public Service Commission. I was not selected, which I did not regret as I wanted to stay on in Bombay. On this occasion, when Bansi's first birthday party was celebrated in Datar's house, I met Ashok Mitra, who has remained a lifelong friend.

I was asked to go as a member of the Indian delegation to an international conference on planning convened in Bangkok by the UN Economic Commission for Asia and the Far East (ECAFE); and to Bangalore in early 1956 as part of the Indian delegation to ECAFE's annual meeting. Though both these were short visits, they were my first experience of international conferences and delegation constraints, which came in handy later. Soon after my return from Bangalore, the World Bank wrote to the RBI, requesting my services for a couple of years on deputation. The Bank agreed to let me go, much to my surprise. It is still a mystery who or what caused this change in the Bank's attitude.

4

An Academic Interlude

LOOKING back on our first trip to Washington DC in 1956, it is amazing how much has changed since then. We are now so used to jet planes, multiple carriers, huge, crowded airports, fast travel, humiliating security checks and so on that we can hardly visualise how leisurely and enjoyable air travel was those days. One thing, however, has remained unchanged – the unearthly hours of arrival in or departure from India. For the rest, the extent of change has been truly remarkable. In the mid-1950s, Air-India had a virtual monopoly of air travel from out of Bombay. The terminal was a converted hangar, flights were few, procedures simple and the crowds were meagre. We boarded the aircraft within minutes of checking in; it was a big four-engine propeller plane. My wife, daughter and I travelled first class in great comfort, including sleeping berths. It was a long flight to London, with frequent re-fuelling stops. After a brief stay in London, we boarded a similar aircraft in the evening and with a changeover in New York, reached Washington DC by lunch time the next day.

In Washington, we repaired quickly to the hotel where we had reservations. It was a Saturday, in mid-August; the morning was bright and warm and we felt no discomfort weather-wise. P S N Prasad, formerly the RBI's economic adviser and at that time, India's executive director at the IMF, took us home for lunch, where we met his wife and daughters, all of whom virtually adopted us as their family. It was a connection which grew fonder as time passed and has flourished over the years. Very similar was our experience with Alec Cairncross and his family. Alec was the director of the Economic Development Institute (EDI) of the World Bank, which had just been set up and my appointment was as a teaching member at the EDI. Thanks to the Prasad and Cairncross families, our initial days in Washington DC turned out to be less difficult than we feared; it certainly helped in familiarising us with the city and its culture.

Washington in the late 1950s was very different from Bombay. As we discovered in the next couple of weeks, it was more like New Delhi, with broad avenues, plenty of greenery, and historic monuments, but by and large a "government" city. Alec drove us around, showing us the city's principal landmarks, the White House and the lovely stretch from the Capitol to Lincoln Memorial, the Tidal Basin and the Potomac river, museums and the Smithsonian Institute. It was also, like Delhi, a city of contrasts with stately houses and apartments in the northern half where the whites lived. The southern quarters were inhabited mostly by African Americans, with patently run-down houses and crowded tenements poorly maintained. Elsewhere, in hotels and shops, there was clear discrimination on a colour basis. This became apparent as we went around looking for an apartment in the northern half. Ultimately, we found one on 16th Street NW, which was only a couple of streets away from the "black" area. That we were Indians and my wife wore a sari probably helped. The Birmingham protests and Martin Luther King were still many years away for African-Americans to establish their equality before law.

The apartment we leased on 16th Street NW was within walking distance of the EDI. The institute was still in a formative stage, having tried out only an experimental course before I joined. Its main objectives were to bring together senior-level government officers of the World Bank's developing country members, and to familiarise them with the basic tenets of development economics and related policies. Besides me and the director, there were three other members of the teaching staff who had been seconded by the Bank, one from its economics department and the others from its country and administrative departments. Alec, a distinguished economist from the UK, had served in his country's government during the war years as an adviser and so was familiar with the ways of bureaucracies. The little villa in which the EDI was housed consisted of a spacious lounge and maintenance facilities on the ground floor, a fair-sized seminar room, library and offices for all of us upstairs. The participants in the next course, which was to start in October 1956, were housed in a hotel very near the institute.

A week or so after I joined, we had a meeting at which the draft syllabus for a course of six months was discussed. This was subsequently approved by a committee consisting of the Bank's president, vice-presidents, economic adviser, Alec and departmental heads. The course was to run from October to March each year, including breaks for Christmas and a couple of field visits. Not all the seminars in the course had to be conducted by the EDI's permanent faculty. Visiting faculty from the Bank and the IMF as well as universities and other institutions were brought in to address the participants. All this was decided in time for us to prepare the brief notes and reading materials to be distributed to the participants every week for each day's sessions.

Since the participants had long ceased to be students and were not accustomed to hard study, we had to figure out the best means of ensuring that they really benefited from the course. It was up to us to ensure that they did not lose interest in the seminars or other related activities included in their programme. Apart from week-long field trips to places of interest, the EDI course consisted of visits to the World Bank's various departments, the IMF and the Federal Reserve Board. Special lectures by distinguished visitors and other eminent persons from the Bank's member countries were also arranged in the institute. This was necessary not merely because of the institute's limited staff but also to prevent the participants from getting bored by the same old faces. In reality, these breaks greatly enriched the value of the participants' experience. For each seminar, we scheduled an introductory talk on the subject, followed by a discussion. Along with some reading material, a brief resume of the lecture was provided to the participants. For seminars by visiting lecturers, one or more of us sat in and assisted in the ensuing discussion of the topic. And as many of us as possible made ourselves available to the participants in case they needed some assistance later. As part of the programme, we also arranged social events in the institute, during which refreshments and entertainment were provided. Several Bank and IMF staff members were usually invited to these evening sessions. Such informal sessions helped the participants to meet them and sort out any questions they may have had relating to their countries.

Because of my experience in the PC and the RBI, I was asked to conduct the seminars on national income analysis, monetary questions, development issues and some basic macro-analysis. My economist colleague from the Bank dealt with investment criteria, foreign trade and payments, project evaluation, and World Bank and IMF policies relating to growth and stability. Others, including the director, handled case studies from both developed and developing countries, questions of policy as well as projects, institutional arrangements for financing development and so on. All these sessions aimed at enabling the participants to sort out the relevant from the irrelevant and the feasible from the non-feasible when they received advice from their economic or technical advisers. In essence, the courses were tailored to assist bureaucrats to contribute effectively to their countries' development. If, in the process, they learnt some development economics, that was okay; but it was more a by-product of the course rather than its main purpose. Altogether, the EDI was viewed by the Bank as well as by its staff as an educational enterprise and what the participants gained from it depended wholly on their specific interests and efforts.

The participants were from the developing countries of Africa, Asia as well as Europe, not all of which were at peace with one another, or even within themselves. Besides India and Pakistan, there were Turkey and Iran, Israel and Egypt, which were actually or virtually at war with each other. There were also countries like Yugoslavia, which had serious internal disagreements, or Japan and Korea with bitter memories. However, despite the apprehensions of the World Bank and the EDI staff, no fights or major disputes arose among participants. Perhaps it helped that they all lived together in the same hotel, or that they were bureaucrats who had learnt to serve different masters. They of course argued fiercely with one another on all manner of issues – political, cultural, even religious; their food habits varied; some were hard drinkers and others teetotallers; even so, they were at peace and often developed fast friendships. But throughout the course, the director and his associates were anxious to see that nothing untoward happened.

My stint with the EDI came at a time when India's – and Prime Minister Nehru's – reputation abroad was very high. Both had weathered successfully the trauma of Partition and the huge problem of resettlement of refugees, held two general elections, embarked on five-year plans and contributed in good measure to the work of the UN and its associate institutions. Despite the pessimistic prognostications of British and other scribes, the country had not only held together but also laid the firm foundations for a democratic polity. True enough, economic progress after independence was limited and poverty was acute and extensive. Neither Americans nor Europeans were happy with India's "non-alignment" policy in foreign affairs or with its friendly relations at that time with the USSR and China. Altogether, India and Indians were well thought of, and people (in Washington DC at least) were eager to know more about them.

By the time I reached Washington, the First Five-Year Plan had been completed and the Second Five-Year Plan had been elaborated. Underlying this Plan was the notable draft of a multi-sector model prepared by Mahalanobis, which aroused considerable controversy in India and elsewhere. Principally, the framework of the Second Plan envisaged massive investment in basic and capital goods industries, involving, among others, resorting to sizeable deficit financing. Neither the IMF nor the World Bank seemed happy with the basic approach of the PC and India's executive directors at these organisations had a difficult time coping with the plethora of questions raised in the meetings of their respective boards. While the IMF was not pleased with the recourse to deficit financing as well as the drawdown of foreign assets by India, the World Bank did not like large investments by the government sector in heavy industries and the relative neglect of consumer goods, including agriculture. My colleagues in the EDI were likewise eager to understand more fully the logic behind India's Plans, and I found myself in the somewhat piquant situation of having to explain things in both the Bank and the EDI. Fortunately, the common Bank-Fund library contained most of the PC documents, on the basis of which I could prepare my notes on India's approach to development.

One serious problem in all this was the total lack of knowledge about India at all levels of the Bank and the Fund. Most of them had no conception of the depth of Indian poverty, nor of the poor state of education and health facilities, or of the lack of infrastructure. There was hardly any understanding of the dilemmas the newly set-up governments in India had to face, nor of the immensity of its development needs. The paucity of economic statistics and the US' total dependence on the UK for reports on India further hindered a proper understanding of India's economic and social problems. There was also a tilt in the US government towards Pakistan, largely due to India's non-alignment policy. Altogether, it was not entirely easy to operate in Washington DC at that juncture.

There was a further issue. At that time, the World Bank was very much free-market oriented and "planning" on a national scale was not an activity that it sought to encourage. It operated essentially in terms of project finance; and the projects that it preferred to finance were expected to be commercially viable rather quickly. What India had embarked on in its Second Five-Year Plan were long-gestation projects in steel, heavy machinery and other basic industries in the public sector, for which it had secured some assistance from the Soviet, German and British governments. In this climate, the going was initially a bit tough for me. But over a period, things got better as the US government and others collaborated to set up the International Development Association (IDA) under the auspices of the World Bank to extend "soft loans" to developing countries, mainly for investment in road and railway projects, irrigation dams and similar enterprises involving very substantial local expenditure. Even here, the preference was more for material construction activity than for social infrastructure such as education and health, facilities which were vital for the majority of Indians. Altogether, the contents of India's Second Five-Year Plan were not something which the World Bank liked. Even so, my colleagues at the EDI felt that it was important for them as well as the participants to understand the circumstances under which India had embarked on this strategy, and that I should deal with this issue fully in my seminars. Though the USSR and communist China were not members of the Fund or the World Bank, the academics in Washington were vastly interested in their economic and technological developments, which also eased my task to some extent.

The process of preparing seminar notes and readings also benefited me personally. Primarily, the task of clarifying to others the philosophy behind India's five-year plans helped me to understand more fully the theory of the "big-push" in the development context. In the Second Five-Year Plan, heavy investment on basic and capital goods industries as well as on power and other infrastructure activities were based on the strong backward and forward linkages of these, together with the promise of technological benefits. That they all involved heavy capital outlays was, indeed, an issue of relevance to a capital-scarce (or labour-surplus) country. However, this was to be countered by the country's willingness to obtain foreign aid from international institutions as well as foreign governments and by raising the rate of domestic savings from the new incomes generated during the Plan period. In theory, at any rate, these were plausible expectations in India; and so were they for most of the participants from developing countries.

Within the World Bank and IMF, there was much scepticism on the availability of adequate aid for government-dominated projects. However, there was very considerable interest in India's experiment with macro-planning under conditions of co-existence with a substantial private sector producing wage goods. This was being undertaken in a democratic polity with a written constitution and clear separation of powers between the legislative, executive and judicial authorities. On the whole, it was an experiment in which the World Bank and the EDI were much interested – a circumstance that helped somewhat.

Besides the setting up of the IDA as part of the World Bank, another incident turned out to be beneficial in some ways. In the late 1950s, the annual Bank-Fund conference of governors was organised in New Delhi. For many of the senior and middle-level officials of the two institutions, it was their first visit to India; most of them came back with an altered conception of the enormity of mass poverty in India, and the compulsions on the central and state governments to seek rapid economic progress. One such was Robert Garner, who at that time was the vice-president in charge of the International Finance Corporation of the World Bank, a body specially designed to assist private enterprises seeking foreign equity or loans. Soon after returning from the New Delhi conference, he telephoned me to meet him in his office. When I went there, the first thing he said was that he had absolutely no conception of what real poverty meant and that his visit to some parts of India had enabled him to understand how acute and extensive was the deprivation of the poor. He also seemed to understand how urgent the need was to improve their living conditions. The visit to India was for him an eye-opener, as it was to many others in the twin institutions, and to other foreign governments at the conference. Suddenly, there was a plethora of requests for the Bank's reports on India, as also for the materials we had prepared at the EDI for the participants.

A question which frequently came up during the seminars at the EDI was that of massive rural unemployment in India, especially from African participants. In most of their countries, they faced similar situations, though in many of them poverty did not necessarily imply starvation or malnutrition. The participants were aware of the difference in the man-land ratios of India on the one hand and their countries on the other. However, they recognised that agriculture's contribution to the GDP in India at that stage was substantial, and that productivity per man-day or per acre was low. Any improvement in this implied the shifting of surplus labour from land, and the question was where they would find steady jobs. This was a matter of considerable importance to the participants and they were naturally interested in India's Plans. The Second Five-Year Plan had provided for massive investment in the basic and capital goods sector, which was capital, not labour, intensive. It was in the small- and medium-scale consumer goods industries that the Plan expected greater use of labour-intensive technologies. This may have been logical, but not necessarily convincing to either the participants or my colleagues at the EDI. While some questioned the capacity of the small-scale sector to adequately step up the supply of consumer goods, others doubted the willingness of farmers to give up their land and move over to non-farm occupations. This was especially true of tribals, whose customs and lifestyles were fully attuned to their natural environment. Were things very different with Indian farmers, they asked. While recognising the strength of this argument, I tried to suggest that support to village and small-scale industries under India's Second Five-Year Plan was intended to enlarge the opportunities for non-farm employment in rural areas. However, this was not something which the participants found convincing. As things turned out later, they were right and the Indian government's policy had to be modified.

Like the "public-private" controversy between India and the developed countries of Europe and America, another issue at that juncture was India's emphasis on import-substitution for industrial diversification. A large part of India's industrial investment in the mid-1950s was directed towards domestic production of internationally traded goods, such as steel, chemicals and fertilisers, as well as machinery, to displace imports. Very little attention was paid to cost-effective production of exports for which India had some natural advantage such as agricultural and industrial raw materials. The emphasis on import substitution derived partly from the desire to promote structural modification through heavy industrial investment and partly from the desire to avoid having to secure foreign aid or loans on expensive terms – economically or politically. It was not until much later that this situation changed as a result of developments in India as well as the rest of the world. But in the late 1950s, India had good reasons to pursue the strategy exemplified by the Second Five-Year Plan, and to adhere to its policy of "non-alignment". At the EDI, I remained very much a macro-planner; and the few years of contact with the World Bank or the US did not change my views on what would be good for India.

However, those years greatly helped me see the need for countries in Asia and Africa to achieve much higher rates of growth one way or another, much faster technological progress and more rapid expansion of both general and technical education. Towards these ends, the developing countries could in principle draw on the material and human resources of the advanced economies through both foreign aid and foreign trade. But it was a period of intense cold war between the western democracies and the communist countries, which in turn hampered timely or full contribution to the development of poorer countries by the UN and its functional agencies. While the World Bank and the IMF did not suffer from this problem at the executive level, they nevertheless suffered from the dominance of the US and Europe in decision-making. Governmental assistance by these countries was also meagre. This was striking in the 1950s and perhaps the 1960s as well, and it was only much later that arrangements for more extensive development assistance were forthcoming to Asian and African countries.

This apart, much of a personal nature happened to us before we returned to Bombay and the RBI. Besides visits with EDI participants to New York and a few other cities of interest to them, we went on our own to several places of historic or tourist interest such as Gettysburg, Boston and Harvard, the Niagara Falls and the Shenendoa Valley – mostly by car. After one such trip, I had a bad auto accident, which laid me low for some weeks. We also had a son, Vikram, a few months before we were due to leave on the journey to India. When the World Bank office told us that we could either fly back or take a leisurely sea voyage, we chose the latter, largely because of the chance to travel by the *QE2* across the Atlantic. It did not, however, turn out enjoyable because my wife was seasick part of the way; and when she recovered, our new-born son fell seriously ill and we almost lost him on the way. However, we managed to land in Bombay after about three weeks, all four of us. Despite all this, our sojourn in Washington was a rewarding experience in several ways, for it gave me an opportunity both to teach and learn at the same time. Besides making several enduring friendships with colleagues in the Bank as well as distinguished social scientists visiting the institute, my wife and daughter were able to develop friendships which have been lifelong. As an individual as well as an accomplished musician, my wife was very popular both in the Bank and the Indian community and this added to our enjoyment. That I had a stint with the World Bank also turned out later to be very helpful to me professionally. While all this was to the good, there was one disappointment. The RBI treated my three weeks on the ship as some sort of leave before my joining duty and I could hardly spend a few days with my family in Mysore after having been away for nearly three years. Within a week of seeing my wife and children home, I was back in Bombay. However, there was some compensation; a newly built flat in Colaba was allotted to me. When Madhura and the children came over, I could take them to a brand new apartment.

5

Some Aspects of Industrial Finance

I

IN the mid-1950s, the Shroff Committee on Finance for the Private Sector recommended special agencies for providing equity or long-term loans to the private industrial sector for new investment. One such was the RCI. This was owned partly by the RBI and partly by commercial banks; it used the counterpart funds from US PL-480 assistance for refinancing commercial bank loans to industrial enterprises. Later, it became the Industrial Development Bank of India (IDBI), managed initially by a deputy governor of the RBI. At the time of my return from the EDI in 1959, the RCI was very much a part of the RBI. I was posted as deputy chief officer in the industrial finance department, of which the RCI was a part, a position which gave me an opportunity to deal with industrial finance and its ramifications.

Apart from the SBI, which was taken over and specifically directed by the RBI to enlarge the proportion of its direct lending to agriculturists, much of commercial banking was in the private sector; and as mentioned earlier, these banks were mostly engaged in providing short-term finance to commercial or industrial enterprises. Some state governments had set up SFCs under their auspices to provide medium- to long-term loans to small and medium enterprises. They were modelled on the central government-owned IFCI, and they more or less specialised in lending to industries processing agricultural raw materials or marketing the products of craft enterprises. The RCI was required to provide refinance principally to the SFCs, which were subject to the industrial finance department's supervision. It was also required to provide refinance to commercial banks, which were encouraged to enlarge their medium-term loans to large-scale, organised industries.

The RCI had been set up by the RBI as a private limited company, with its own board of directors, of which a deputy governor was chairman, and representatives of the SBI, the Life Insurance Corporation of India (LIC) and a few of the major commercial banks were members. Apart from the subscribed capital of Rs 12.5 crore, the RCI received a long-term loan of Rs 26 crore from the PL-480 counterpart funds through the Government of India. Because of its limited resources, and the recent origin of medium-term lending by commercial banks, the corporation's refinancing of the SBI and other commercial banks was limited to specific amounts. Similarly, the extent of on-lending to SFCs was also subject to limits, often with the secondary liability of the state government concerned.

Because of the prevailing dogma of banking institutions that those who borrow short cannot afford to lend long, the RCI's initial lending to banks or term-lending institutions like SFCs was very limited. It became necessary by 1961 to liberalise its operations somewhat, by providing for foreign currency loans against rupee repayments to private companies through institutions like the ICICI (which had access to the International Finance Corporation of the World Bank, the Commonwealth Development Finance Corporation of the UK, and the like). Arrangements were also made to enlarge the quantum of assistance that could be extended jointly by financial institutions to small-scale businesses which were covered by the newly constituted Credit Guarantee Scheme.

Though I joined the industrial finance department in February 1959, it was the credit guarantee of loans to small-scale industries rather than enlarging the operations of the RCI that became my main task, largely due to the deep concern of deputy governor B Venkatappiah with the development of agriculture and the small-industries sector in rural India. He had found the SBI's experimental scheme of lending to small-scale industries through its rural branches a creative operation. He believed that other commercial banks, urban co-operative banks and other financial institutions could follow the SBI example with advantage, provided the risks involved could be shared in some way.

It was at this juncture that Venkatappiah got me involved in the task of persuading the Government of India to share the risks of long-term loans to small-scale industries and businesses. At his behest, the Bank's departments of research and statistics had examined international experience in this and made a variety of suggestions, which he asked me to study and report back to him. There were actually two separate questions involved. Many smaller banks and urban co-operatives were willing to lend and supervise long-term loans to small businesses. But they lacked the financial capability of extending such loans to several small borrowers and spreading their risks. Nor could they resort to the other means of sharing the risk with somebody else. Though there were agencies like the RBI, the SBI or the National Small Industries Corporation (NSIC) from which refinance could be obtained for some of the better-secured small industry loans, there were no agencies with which to share the risk as such. It was the latter question which I was asked to examine.

This was within a few weeks of my joining the industrial finance department, and Venkatappiah's instructions were that the whole gamut of problems involved in a credit guarantee scheme should be quickly worked out. He wanted the relevant issues to be discussed in a wide-ranging seminar involving not only the banks and other financial agencies concerned, but also the Ministry of Finance and the development commissioner for small industries in New Delhi; directors of industries of state governments; chambers of commerce and industry; and so forth. This was to take place in July 1959 and I had all of three months to come up with a viable scheme.

Meantime, within the RBI a decision had yet to be taken whether the RBI Act permitted its taking on a credit guarantee function – which the Bank's legal department did not think was allowed. While this was being debated, I went over to New Delhi to discuss various issues with the Ministry of Finance and the office of the development commissioner as well as with persons like P N Dhar at the Delhi School of Economics, who had studied the problems of small-scale industries in Okhla, Faridabad and other areas in the capital's vicinity. At the Finance Ministry, R K Seshadri, a deputy secretary, was assigned to discuss matters with me. He was in any event dealing with questions connected with RBI operations, including how the SFCs could be backstopped. Seshadri was a very meticulous person and his association with the credit guarantee question turned out to be a great help. We went over for a detailed discussion with the development commissioner, who favoured a new institution to provide such guarantee facilities, supported by the Government of India as well as the

RBI. Further, he wished that along with small-scale industries, some service industries like road transport be included in any future scheme. However, there was no agreement on what kind of institutional arrangement would best serve the purpose in terms of both adequacy of finance and speed of operation. This, along with such specific questions as the extent of risk coverage, and private industries or businesses to be covered, was left for detailed discussion at the proposed seminar.

The seminar, which was held in Hyderabad in July 1959, had a detailed agenda and was presided over by Venkatappiah, who desired that it should produce very specific proposals on how exactly the small-scale sector should be helped, what role organised financial institutions should play, who (if any) should provide marketing or insurance assistance, and so on. After a couple of days of exhaustive (and exhausting) discussion, it was agreed that (a) commercial banks, SFCs and co-operative banks should all be encouraged to lend to the small-scale sector; (b) a specific scheme for sharing the risk involved in such lending should be put in place; (c) small industries service institutes and directors of industries in state governments should supervise such credit; and (d) the precise extent of coverage, charges to be levied and so on should be left to the decision of the guaranteeing institution. It was also the general opinion at the seminar that the decision on the agency guaranteeing the credit risk should be taken by the Government of India in consultation with the RBI.

Ultimately, it was decided that a credit guarantee scheme should be operated by the RBI through its industrial finance department. This became effective in July 1960, after the RBI Act was amended to enable it to function as an agent of the Government of India, which was to bear the financial burden. Under this scheme, the RBI could guarantee the loans given to small industries and businesses by the SBI, its associate banks, most of the scheduled commercial banks, state co-operative banks and SFCs. Loans to such enterprises having capital investment of up to Rs 5 lakh were eligible for guarantee. The risks of financial institutions were normally covered up to 50 per cent, subject to an upper limit to the amount involved. In exceptional cases, 75 per cent of the risk could be covered. A comprehensive review of the scheme was to be undertaken after two years of its working, and a decision taken on whether or not to continue it.

Virtually all my time as an officer in the industrial finance department was taken up in implementing the scheme, in which task Seshadri provided invaluable support. He was, from the beginning, less enthusiastic about it than Venkatappiah or the staff of the department for various reasons. His scepticism derived essentially from two general characteristics of the small- and medium industries sector. Most such industries were either proprietary partnerships or private limited companies; they were generally "registered" companies, subject to inspection by state governments. However, most of them tended to be poorly organised, without proper maintenance of inventories, accounts and the like, all required of them. It was often difficult to find out how exactly the loan amount had been utilised, how sales proceeds had been taken into account, or how a cost-price relationship had been worked out. A second major difficulty was that despite the reservation of markets or price preferences in governments' procurement policies, their marketing arrangements remained unsatisfactory. Seshadri strongly held that unless these issues were properly addressed, mere sharing of the risk would not help in enlarging the credit extended to them by banks, and that, for the most part, such a facility would encourage these institutions to recall their loans and drive small industries to seek the assistance of private moneylenders or traders.

As the scheme went into operation in a limited number of districts to start with, not many banks came up for guarantee, with the exception of the SBI and its associate banks. This may have been because of their wider network of branches or the larger amounts lent by them or their closeness to the RBI. Whatever the reason, applications for guarantee from this group of banks far exceeded those from other scheduled banks. SFCs had mostly specialised in loans up to seven years and thus were technically ineligible to seek RBI guarantee. Not many state co-operative banks came up for assistance at that stage for whatever reason. The relatively slow growth of guarantees sought by small-scale industrial units contrasted with those sought by lorry operators, especially those owning one or a few such vehicles. Altogether, the pressure of guarantee work was not very taxing in the initial months and considerable time was left to me and my colleagues in the industrial finance department to streamline operations and discuss each request in detail with the banks concerned.

II

However, in early 1960, I was drafted for other work and it was not until many years later that I had a chance to revisit the credit guarantee scheme. By then, the industrial finance department had disappeared. Its functions relating to the corporate sector had been taken over by the IDBI and a new Credit Guarantee Corporation of India had come into being, within the RBI family.

What diverted my attention in 1960 were two important World Bank missions with which I was associated, along with an economist in the Ministry of Finance, Sharad Marathe. The Government of India wanted us to accompany these missions during their Indian visit, and provide whatever factual or other assistance they may need. The first of these was the so-called "Wise Men Mission" consisting of Oliver Franks of the UK, Herman Abs of West Germany and Allan Sproul of the US. They were to spend about three weeks in India, meeting ministers and officials of governments, PC members, the RBI and the SBI, some corporate executives and so forth, and provide the World Bank with a general assessment of the economic and political conditions in India at the end of the Second Plan period. Franks was very much a don, a gentleman scholar of the Oxbridge type, very polite and more eager to listen than offer comments on what he had observed or heard. The other two were cast in a different mould. Abs obviously felt very self-important and was often aggressive in dealing with others. With a banker's background, he tended to lay down the line rather than discuss issues with an open mind. Heavy and florid of complexion, Abs had the aspect of a wine merchant rather than a banker, without of course the former's amiability. Sproul was slight of build and sallow of skin, but as conscious of his importance as his colleague from Germany and commented all the time on how sloppy the Indians were. It was altogether not a happy three weeks that Sharad and I spent with these "wise men," before they went across to Pakistan, on which also they had to report to the World Bank. What exactly came out of their reports was not clear to us then or later. It was, however, believed that they recommended the need for providing sizeable, long-term assistance to both India and Pakistan, and that the World Bank should take the lead in systematising such help, to be given collectively by the Bank's member-governments rather than individually in a haphazard manner. The Aid-India (and Aid Pakistan) consortium was perhaps the visible outcome of the mission.

Before the World Bank embarked on this step, it decided to send a regular "Bank Mission" for an assessment of India's foreign aid requirements for the Third Five-Year Plan, which was to commence in April 1961. This was led by Michael Hoffman, who had succeeded Alec as director of the EDI in 1957. Having known me at the EDI, he particularly wanted me to be associated with his mission and negotiated with the government as well as the RBI for my release to join the mission as an adviser. This was to be for a somewhat longer period of four to six weeks and involved a series of discussions with the PC, various ministries, business associations, the RBI and the major banks, state governments and so forth. The Hoffman Mission was to visit many state capitals, industrial locations, ports and port authorities in different parts of the country, all of which were necessitated by the diversity of India's economy, politics and society. Accompanying the Mission, I could see many parts of India which I had not visited and appreciate more fully the diversity of people constituting the Indian Union and their problems.

The provocation for the Hoffman Mission, following that of the "three wise men," arose from two general presumptions on the size as well as strategy of the soon-to-start Third Five-Year Plan. The Government of India was under pressure from the ruling Congress Party (as well as many liberal intellectuals) to strive to move rapidly towards assuring certain "minimum standards of living" for the mass of Indian people in the next five-year plan. I believe that the party desired to please as large a section of the electorate as possible because it had to face a general election in 1962. It also wanted at the same time to achieve a significant structural modification of India's economy, through massive industrial investment. However, experience during the Second Five-Year Plan had made it clear that India's domestic savings were not large enough to sustain both more agricultural investment (without which the minimum standards objective could not be attained) and a big increase in investment in the industrial sector. It was clear that without a substantial draft on foreign savings, the strategy of the Second Five-Year Plan could not be continued in the 1960s. This was also the substance of the wise-men mission, which had gone a step further and recommended that the World Bank should take a lead in this matter, especially after it had assumed managerial responsibility for the International Development Association. It is against this background that the Hoffman Mission was to assess in some detail India's likely requirement of foreign aid, indicating how much of it could be in the form of bankable loans and how much as grants or soft loans.

During the course of the Mission, it became clear that there were differences between the Indian government and state governments on the one hand and the World Bank on the other. While the central government favoured continued emphasis on heavy investment in the public sector on basic industries, the state governments, which had a constitutional responsibility for agriculture and social services like education, health and community facilities, favoured larger Plan expenditures on these items. State governments could share their heavy responsibilities for agriculture and other services with private enterprise if they could be given some aid and assistance. This question of relative weights to be attached to the public and private sectors was also a matter of some disagreement with the World Bank. However, with the Hoffman Mission, this was not a big issue; it became more acrimonious with the next Bank Mission (of which later).

Despite these differences, when Hoffman and his team left India, they had pretty much been sold the principal contents of the Third Plan. The Plan was built on an expectation of a higher inflow of foreign assistance than had been secured for the Second Plan. For the Third Plan, the Mission had been informed that for both the public sector and private sector, a Plan outlay of a little over Rs 10,000 crore (over the five-year period) may need foreign assistance of around 20 per cent, excluding loan repayments and drawing on PL 480 rupee counterparts. The Bank Mission was concerned about the extent of deficit financing envisaged over the five-year period; in financing the Second Plan, the government had incurred budget deficits of nearly Rs 1,000 crore, which together with supply difficulties had led to a significant increase in food prices. At that stage, the thinking in the PC was that with some additional effort, aggregate domestic savings could be stepped up from about 9 per cent of GDP to about 12 per cent by the end of the Third Plan period. It was also thought that with some restraint on production of, and expenditure on, non-essential goods and services, the domestic prices of commodities of common consumption could be prevented from going up further. Altogether, as I sat in at the meetings the Hoffman Mission had with the Government of India and state governments, I had the feeling that in framing the Third Plan a very significant effort had been made to avoid undue pressure on domestic prices as also balance of payments on the one hand and linking financial outlays to achievable domestic real resources on the other. On the availability of foreign assistance of the required order, much depended on the Hoffman Mission's recommendations to the World Bank and the Aid-India consortium.

By the time foreign-aid givers could meet and take a view on India's Third Plan requirements, conditions in the country worsened in several respects. Communal disturbances, occupation of the Portuguese enclaves of Goa, Diu and Daman, and, above all, intensification of the border dispute with China led to growing unease. Foreign scholars and news reporters from abroad visiting or stationed in India grew openly pessimistic about the prospects of democracy as well as the danger of conflict with China. The general election of 1962 had only slightly weakened Nehru's Congress; but Nehru himself had grown frail and tired. Within a few months of the end of 1961, the border conflict with China became serious and impaired India's standing in the world. For good or bad reasons, there was a delay in the World Bank pledging any aid for the Third Plan on the basis of the Hoffman Mission recommendations.

Meanwhile, things were happening in New Delhi. Within the PC, there was an intense debate on how the strategy of heavy investment on basic and capital goods industries could be combined effectively, with the "minimum standards of living" objective for which political pressure had developed. By 1960, it had become clear that sizeable additions to the cultivated area were no longer possible and an increase in agricultural output could only be achieved through higher productivity. It was also obvious that expanding the production of wage goods (other than food stuffs) through support to small-scale industries in the rural sector had not been successful in the Second Plan period. As mentioned earlier, preliminary estimates of investment requirements for the Third Plan period showed clearly that any significant step-up in investment required more inflow of foreign assistance, or more export of domestic products, besides resort to deficit financing. A series of policy conflicts had thus surfaced and the Commission had to necessarily re-examine the Second Plan strategy more thoroughly than it had assumed. About the same time, Anjaria, who was doubling up as economic adviser to the PC in addition to being chief economic adviser to the Ministry of Finance, was asked to go to Washington as executive director for India on the IMF. Before he left the PC, he requested the RBI to send me on deputation to head a new division on economic policy and growth which the PC had decided to set up to examine the variety of policy options open to it. The PC wanted to ensure that the momentum for structural and technological changes built up in the Second Plan period was not weakened. After considerable discussion and delay, my deputation to the PC for an unspecified period was accepted by the RBI in late 1961.

6

Back Again to Delhi

I

IT was almost a decade later that I was returning to New Delhi, to a new office and a new home. The city had grown much bigger and busier, though the old landmarks continued to dominate the skyline and greenery abounded. The PC had moved into a building of its own, Yojana Bhavan on Parliament Street, symbolically midway between government offices to the south and the business centre of Connaught Place to the north. The apartment allotted to me by the government was a few kilometres to the south, past the Diplomatic Enclave. Some of my friends from the LSE and the PC had continued to live and prosper in New Delhi. It did not take long for me to settle down in the office or in the city.

The PC had in the meantime grown in size and stature. G L Nanda (who was the deputy chairman in the early 1950s) had come back to his old position but the rest of the commission consisted of new full-time members as well as some Cabinet ministers besides the Finance Minister. In particular, Mahalanobis had moved up to full membership of the PC, and Defence Minister Krishna Menon had been brought in by the Prime Minister. Both of them were strong advocates of state planning, having been more impressed by the Soviet Union than the US. At the official level, Tarlok Singh was virtually the PC's Secretary, in charge of administration and plan co-ordination. The economic division had been trifurcated and it took some time for the chiefs of other divisions to accept my entry. Somewhat to my advantage, Pitambar Pant, chief of the perspective planning division, who was reputed to be close to the Prime Minister, befriended me early and took me along to meet several distinguished economists and statisticians who were in the Delhi branch of the ISI. Within a couple of weeks, I was able to go around the few ministries with which we were to discuss matters of sectoral policy and arrangements for project preparation and evaluation. These visits also helped me to establish good working relations with their technical personnel.

Considerable thought had been given within the PC to the strategy of long-term growth of the economy, as well as the several targets to be achieved. These were more or less along the same lines as in the Second Plan, and my initial concern was to know in some detail what had (or had not) been achieved under that Plan. In the early 1960s, it was possible to undertake an analysis of the trends and fluctuations in different components of the aggregate economy, on the basis of data available from the CSO or the initial rounds of the National Sample Survey (NSS). My work in the RBI had given me some appreciation of the link between real and financial magnitudes as also the nature of the corporate sectors of industry, trade and finance. What was new in the PC's work was co-ordinating the central Plan with the state Plans to visualise the likely stresses and strains at the fiscal level. In this conjuncture, I found my task of elucidating the growth process and deriving the policy alternatives a formidable one. This was somewhat awkward for two reasons. Primarily, Pitambar Pant as head of the perspective planning division and his proximity to the Prime Minister's office, could secure more details of projects or proposals generated by the different ministries in New Delhi and elsewhere. He also had access through the ISI to more details of national income than others. Thus he tended to dominate inter-divisional or inter-ministerial meetings of the PC. Second, not having become the economic adviser to the commission with Anjaria's departure, I could not fully secure the co-operation of the other division chiefs who were my equals. However, Pitambar Pant was anxious to establish the theoretical consistency of projections of different resource-using sectors of the economy, and sought to work closely with me. He was willing to share basic data with me and my colleagues in the division, and over a period of months, we got to work pretty closely. Recognising this, Tarlok Singh also instructed the other division chiefs to collaborate with us more closely.

In the economic policy and growth division we discussed how best to chalk out the possible scenarios. In the context of the Second Plan, much advance had been achieved in development theory and strategy, both in India and abroad. The seminal contributions of multi-sector models by Mahalanobis, Raj, Amartya Sen and others in India, and of Simon Kuznets, Arthur Lewis, Walt Rostow and Jan Tinbergen abroad, together with the elucidation of input-output relations by Wassily Leontief, had widened our field of choice substantially. We visualised the preparation of input-output matrices of multiple sectors, based on the somewhat extensive data available from the CSO as well as the NSSO. Pitambar Pant's division was also developing a more detailed input-output matrix based on extensive data available to it from the ISI. This was a hard and time-consuming task, but in early 1962, we could look forward hopefully to articulation of long-term development strategies. Though things turned out to be less favourable in later years, both our divisions kept going as intended.

II

In the later part of 1961-62, even as the PC was settling down to figure out long-term growth prospects, events outside were getting more unsettled. As the border dispute with China grew serious, Nehru's position within the Congress Party weakened somewhat, largely because of his support to Krishna Menon, the Defence Minister. It was generally believed that because of his faith in Chinese friendship, Menon had failed to equip the defence forces adequately in good time to withstand Chinese incursions in the Aksai Chin and Tawang areas. At about the same time, several expectations of the PC on the economic front went awry. Despite some increase in irrigated area, agricultural output had not increased and food prices rose ominously. Much of the foreign exchange reserves had been utilised for the Second Plan projects, which had not come up as expected. In this milieu, the "big push" strategy of the Second Plan, which had largely been followed in the Third Plan, lost some support politically as well as academically. By early 1962, with parliamentary elections in the offing, dissension within the ruling party on policy issues became open and badly affected Nehru's effectiveness. And when later in the year hostilities with China broke out all along the frontier, it seemed likely that the Third Plan would need major adjustments.

Views differed within the PC on how this change in the situation was to be accommodated. Obviously, defence outlays had to be stepped up but the question was how. If the development outlay was to be maintained as before, either more resources had to be mobilised or more deficit-financing resorted to, with inevitable consequences on domestic inflation and the payments deficit. However, the country's foreign exchange resources had already been drawn down heavily, and their further depletion did not appear practicable. Alternatively, more foreign aid had to be sought for both military and Plan purposes. It had also become patent by then that the requirement for the states' part of the Third Plan for investment in agriculture, irrigation and power would be higher than forecast and thus enlarge their draft on the centre's resources. Altogether, intra and inter-governmental differences proliferated and a whole range of issues piled up on the desk of the Prime Minister, as head of the government, as well as of the PC. Meanwhile, there was a setback to Nehru's health and as elections for the Lok Sabha approached, he could hardly pay attention to the dilemmas faced by the PC or the National Development Council. He had to make sure of his party winning a comfortable majority in the Lok Sabha, particularly after the disputes concerning the continuation of Krishna Menon as Defence Minister. Since Krishna Menon was seeking re-election to the Lok Sabha from an important constituency in Bombay, the Prime Minister decided to go to Bombay and several other constituencies to canvas for his party. While all this was going on outside, members and officials of the PC were busy evaluating the country's political and economic alternatives for dealing with external aggression on one side and mass poverty and unemployment on the other. Some, like Pitambar Pant and Mahalanobis, strongly favoured additional resource mobilisation for avoiding a reduction in Plan expenditure. They further argued that since an increased defence outlay would largely be for obtaining equipment from abroad, it would be worthwhile seeking foreign assistance for this purpose. This view was not much favoured by the Finance Ministry, which believed the tax burden on the non-agricultural sectors was already heavy. The Ministry of External Affairs (of which the Prime Minister was the head) was, however, not prepared to seek any military assistance from either the US or the USSR as it would weaken the nation's non-alignment policy.

In these circumstances, my division and I found ourselves in a piquant situation. To us, it was obvious that without massive investment in the heavy industries and infrastructure sectors, no long-term economic development was feasible. It was also clear that domestic inflation could not be controlled without a big increase in agricultural output – or without a heavier import of wage goods. If, in addition, resources for defence expenditure had to be sought, there was no alternative to stepping up domestic savings much beyond what had been projected for Third Plan purposes and seeking more foreign aid from the World Bank or others. By then, it was known that the Hoffman Mission had favoured larger consortium assistance to India's Third Five-Year Plan, including sizeable soft loans through the IDA. I was therefore more or less in agreement with Pitambar Pant that every effort should be made to preserve the projected Plan outlay and also provide more for defence purposes. But the chiefs of the other economic divisions (of public finance and foreign trade and payments) did not see eye to eye with me. The differences persisted until the Prime Minister found it possible to come to Yojana Bhavan for a full meeting of the PC.

The Commission meeting that followed was momentous. By the time the Prime Minister came, all the members and officials who were required to attend were in the conference room. The Secretary waited at the entrance to the building along with a host of Yojana Bhavan employees, who had gathered to see Nehru. As he came in slowly, they raised a cheer which he acknowledged with a wan smile. It was obvious that his travel for election purposes had exhausted him physically and mentally; conserving his energy for the meeting, he moved on slowly, refusing any assistance offered to him by those around, including his private secretary. As he came into the room, we remained standing until he sat down in his chair. The deputy chairman, Nanda, was on his right and Morarji Desai, the Finance Minister, on the left, with others in their assigned seats. Apart from the finance and defence secretaries and Tarlok Singh who were at the main table, the rest of us sat along the walls.

After Nanda introduced all those in the room, the Prime Minister asked Krishna Menon what exactly was happening at the border with China. Krishna Menon said that news from there was bad; the Chinese troops had crossed the border at many points and Indian troops had fallen back to regroup. Sooner or later, they would have to counter attack, the sooner the better. However, this would not be possible unless we re-equipped them fully and provided them with superior armour. We had to quickly find the wherewithal for all this, and in large amounts. He did not see much hope of securing arms from the Soviet Union against China; and he did not wish to approach the US for help for reasons which the Prime Minister was fully aware of. Altogether, he saw no alternative to being prepared to buying defence material from wherever we could. His ministry would give details of all this to the Prime Minister and the Finance Minister in the next few days. The defence secretary added briefly what equipment had been ordered and what it was likely to cost in both rupees and foreign exchange. This led to some general discussion on possible sources for financing the requirements of the Defence Ministry, to all of which the Prime Minister and Finance Minister listened grimly.

The Prime Minister turned to Nanda to enquire what the progress was on the Third Plan. The PC had completed its round of discussions with the states and central ministries on various projects and programmes and had undertaken many firm commitments. Other members and Tarlok Singh then detailed the measures already taken as well as the likely requirements for the initial years of the five-year period. Morarji Desai, who had listened to all this, came in to say that with the inevitable increase in defence outlay (which of course was a matter of urgency), he was not sure where he could mobilise additional rupee or foreign exchange resources. He could try to economise on non-Plan expenditure, but that would be very limited and would not be adequate to provide for the big increase required for defence. With the price and agricultural situations being what they were, he would not be happy to undertake more deficit financing than had already been agreed on. Perhaps there could be some reduction in central assistance to state Plans if they undertook additional taxation or mobilised more small savings. Altogether, as we could not deny our defence forces whatever they needed (and this would be a great deal), he was not sure if the available resources would suffice for an increase in development outlays as envisaged in the Third Plan. This was not something which the PC was looking forward to and as Nanda began to say something, the Prime Minister, who was already looking very tired, said that he had to leave soon and before doing so could he say a few words.

"Not many years ago", said Nehru softly, "we welcomed Mr Chou En Lai as a friend and a co-worker for peace. Today his troops and ours are ranged all along our northern frontier in a bitter fight." This was for all a tragic disappointment. Now that it had happened, he observed, we were honour-bound to safeguard our territories and preserve the freedom which our people had won at a great cost. "We are also honour-bound to provide our jawans everything they need". He paused for a minute and then went on. "However, we have promised our people much more than freedom from foreign aggression; we have promised them many other freedoms, from poverty, disease and ignorance. We have promised them roads, houses, electricity, water – indeed so much more. Can we provide them all these without economic development?" What else can they look forward to, he asked. They were the principal stakeholders in development, as much as its creators. It was not open to the government to deny them this opportunity just because Chou En Lai had created new problems. "Let us go for defence *with* development, and I have not a shadow of doubt that our people will accept all sacrifices to make this twin achievement possible. We have no choice in this matter and we just cannot afford to let our people down." Having said these few words firmly, he looked directly at the Finance Minister, and sat for a minute to let his words sink into all around the table. Then he got up to signal that the meeting was over. (This does not purport to be a verbatim record of what the Prime Minister said at that meeting, but a summary of what all of us understood as his message.)

As the Prime Minister left with his private secretary and Tarlok Singh in tow, the others fell silent, figuring out the full import of what he had said. His last few words still echoed in our ears; did he really say "defence *with* development"? Did Morarji Desai also understand it that way? Did it imply that Nanda and the rest of us in the PC could feel reassured and go ahead with all the projects and programmes in the Third Plan (and beyond)? However, before he left, Morarji Desai observed that he had no indication from the World Bank-led consortium of the external resource likely to be available over the medium term. As for domestic resource mobilisation, his ministry would explore the possibilities and come up with fresh estimates, after providing fully for defence. With that cryptic message, he left the room, and we asked ourselves, did the Finance Minister really agree with the Prime Minister or does he have reservations?

We told ourselves only time would tell what Morarji Desai considered feasible.

III

While the Finance Ministry was exploring ways and means of satisfying the twin requirements of defence and development, the PC got busy with some advance thinking on the Fourth Five-Year Plan, due to start in 1965-66. The Plan co-ordination division put together the progress so far in the different sectors; the perspective planning division and my division set about working out the possible contents and thrusts in a draft Fourth Plan. The available information on the macro situation indicated that some structural modification had indeed taken place in the manufacturing sector. The general index of industrial production (1956=100) had moved up to 120 by the end of 1963, with that for capital goods rising to 170. Impressive as these indices were, we were aware that the progress appeared substantial mainly because of the low base at the start of the Second Plan. However, the growth in consumer non-durables showed no such progress, having gone up by less than 10 per cent in nearly a decade. The position of agriculture was pretty dismal; the index for foodgrains output had actually declined from 87 in 1961-62 to 84 in 1962-63 (1969-70=100). The wholesale price index for foodgrains had moved up from 100 in 1961-62 to 115 in 1963-64, and was hardening further. While the basic and capital goods industries had shown signs of growth, it was clear that the supply of consumer goods, including food, was not keeping pace with requirements. My colleagues in the economic policy and growth division felt that there was a high probability of price inflation, unless conditions in agriculture and consumer goods industries improved substantially. It had by then become clear that there were serious limitations to extending the area under cultivation and any improvement in agricultural output depended solely on enlarging the area under irrigation as well as multiple-cropping. When we discussed these issues with Pitambar Pant and his colleagues, we were able to reach some common conclusions; first, that, in the Fourth Plan, more resources should be provided for irrigation and land development programmes; and second, private consumer expenditure was likely to be subdued because of higher taxation and saving efforts. Obviously, we were still looking at the future with tinted glasses and did not know what reality had in store for us. However, at that point of time, our estimate of the likely situation at the end of the Third Plan was quite optimistic.

Keeping this picture on one side, we set about putting together a set of commodity balances, for foodstuffs, essential raw materials, coal and energy sources and so forth. As work progressed and more primary data became available, we changed over to convert these balances into input-output matrices, separating inter-industry demands from the constituents of final outputs and final demands. With his access to the data sources in the ISI in Calcutta, Pitambar Pant attempted a more elaborate matrix than we could in our division. These exercises became possible as at about that time the first generation of computers had come up in the Indian Institute of Technology (IIT) in Kanpur and at the Atomic Energy Commission (or the Tata Institute of Fundamental Research) in Bombay. The ISI, which had undertaken a series of NSS, had also established an elaborate data processing system, which we could access when necessary. Altogether, though the PC did not have its own computers, we could utilise the facilities in Kanpur and Bombay for processing our matrices, to draw tentative conclusions on possibilities for the Fourth Plan.

Meanwhile, the number of Indian and foreign economists (and other experts) in Delhi for research collaboration or consultation had increased substantially. The ISI had invited several planning experts from the US and Europe in the 1950s; the newly established Delhi School of Economics under Raj had enlarged its faculty to include Amartya Sen and Jagdish Bhagwati (and later Sukhamoy Chakravarty) among others and had provided for visiting professors from abroad. The ISI campus in Delhi (with which the Commission's perspective planning division had close relations) had added scholars like Ashok Rudra, Bhagecha Minhas and T N Srinivasan to its faculty, besides other experts in econometrics, statistical analysis and sampling theory. This was very much unlike the early 1950s (when Anjaria, Raj and I were working on the First Plan) when all we could fall back on were the aggregative Harrod-Domar models of growth, apart of course from the classics of Ricardo, Joseph Schumpeter and some European economists. Since then, development economics had advanced much. Many young economists and statisticians trained in India or abroad had enriched government ministries, other government organisations and set up new centres of social science research. The growing interest in India's planning endeavours led the Ford and Rockefeller foundations from the US establishing units in Delhi dedicated to work on India's development problems. And soon after, the Massachusetts Institute of Technology (MIT) set up a centre under Max Millikan in Delhi to survey possible ways of assisting India in its development effort. By the time we started working on the draft Fourth Plan, there were immense opportunities available to Pitambar Pant and me to discuss questions of strategy or policies with a range of experts in Delhi and elsewhere. Both the NIU in Delhi and the RBI research department's staff had grown and we could utilise their data sources for our studies. By the time the PC met again towards the end of January 1964, Pitambar Pant had a short paper on a plausible dimensional hypothesis for the Fourth Plan and my division had come up with a preliminary estimate of resource availabilities. Though Pitambar Pant and I had not worked together, we had an understanding of the need to maintain the tempo of development initiated during the Third Plan, despite the urgency of an increased defence outlay. Morarji Desai's budget for 1964-65 was due at the end of February, and the PC was anxious that by then he should have an idea of its thinking on likely Plan requirements.

As it happened, Morarji Desai had indeed taken the Prime Minister's injunction to heart and made a valiant effort to step up taxation, cut back on non-development expenditure as much as possible and provide for more domestic borrowing – all of which were expected to meet the bulk of domestic expenditure on Plan projects. However, the uncertainty regarding foreign exchange availability over an extended period remained. Despite the supportive assessment of the Third Plan by the Hoffman Mission, the Bank had made no firm commitments on a medium-term basis. The border dispute between China and India had intervened and the Aid-India Consortium had apparently decided to wait until the issue was resolved one way or another. One reason for this may have been the World Bank's decision to send yet another mission to India headed by Bernard Bell (1964). This was something of a surprise to the Government of India, which was not happy with such frequent investigations by the Bank, which already had with it the reports by the three wise men and Hoffman.

Meanwhile, Asoka Mehta had replaced Nanda as deputy chairman of the PC, which had been reconstituted, with V K R V Rao as member in-charge of agriculture and education, among others. Like many, Rao was unhappy with the dispute with China and hoped the need for larger spending on defence would not adversely affect the development effort. However, we soon discovered that in terms of development strategy, he did not share our enthusiasm for the "big push." With his concern for food and employment security for the rural masses, he was keen on raising agricultural output to a much higher level, if necessary by altering the technology used for agriculture and other rural activities. While he was aware of the industrial thrust of the Second and Third Plans, he was not as committed to it as Pitambar Pant and me. We had therefore to convince him of the possibility of generating more internal and external resources to provide for larger industrial investment and also for the necessary agricultural infrastructure, especially irrigation, land development and rural education. Both Pitambar Pant and I tried to apprise him of the Prime Minister's deep interest in structural modification of the Indian economy, the point of which he appreciated. But he also said that both economically and politically, it was vital that adequate food supplies were available to the Indian people, an issue on which again the Prime Minister was very positive. After a great deal of discussion, he agreed that the two drafts which we had prepared for discussion with the Prime Minister may be taken up at our meeting with him.

It was probably mid-April by the time the Prime Minster could find time for the PC. His health had deteriorated and he had been advised by his doctors to conserve his energy as much as possible. He had significantly cut down his social and formal engagements; even visits to his office in the South Block had become infrequent. For the PC meeting, we were advised to go to Teen Murthi Bhavan; we were also told to be there promptly and speak only when asked to do so. As the Prime Minster walked in slowly, we stood up as always and waited for him to be seated. His private secretary told Asoka Mehta that we would have about an hour and hoped it would suffice.

Asoka Mehta quickly briefed the Prime Minster on the principal features of the two drafts submitted to him. He pointed out that sectoral allocations in the draft Fourth Plan were similar to those in the Second and Third Plans, with the intention of carrying forward the sectoral and technological developments envisaged in the earlier Plans. He added that both domestic and foreign resource requirements had been set out; however, these had to be further discussed with the Finance Ministry as well as aid-givers abroad. Other members also spoke briefly on their plans and programmes for the next five-year period. When it was Rao's turn, he made a strong pitch for agricultural and educational investments to be accorded a high priority, especially agricultural productivity and primary education in rural areas. Having listened to all this quietly, the Prime Minster looked momentarily at his watch and turned to Asoka Mehta to indicate that he wished to say something. There were two messages he wanted to convey; first, the PC may continue to work along the lines indicated in the drafts and hold discussions with the Finance and other ministries; second, he agreed with Rao that agricultural productivity and primary education should be given due emphasis. It took nearly 10 minutes for him to say this, with frequent stops to catch his breath. It was patent that he was very tired. We were anxious to spare him further effort and went out sadly, leaving him still sitting at the big table. That was the last I was to see him alive.

IV

Prime Minister Nehru died on 24 May 1964 and an era died with him. He had been the undisputed leader not only of India but of all non-aligned nations, a leader who was respected the world over. There was considerable speculation on who would, or should, succeed him as prime minister. At Yojana Bhavan, since the prime minister was also chairman of the PC, we were anxious to know who would be anointed. There were many aspirants to this high office. After much discussion, Lal Bahadur Shastri, a staunch Gandhian and a confidant of Nehru, was chosen by the Congress Party, a decision which surprised many. Shastri was small built and not given to seeking publicity or power. As the Minister for Railways under Nehru, he had resigned from the Cabinet after a bad railway accident, taking the blame on himself for lives lost and damage to public property. Apart from the central government's loss of face following the Chinese invasion, it had also lost some power as a result of differences among senior members of the Congress Party. We naturally waited with anxiety to see how the new Prime Minister would take control of things.

Some time before the new Prime Minister met the PC, my wife had to suddenly go to her hometown because of her father's death; I had admired my father-in-law and would have gone with her if I could. But I was asked to stay on as the Prime Minister had yet to decide to meet the PC. When she was away, it was lonely in the big house and I asked Manu Shroff, who had to move out of his rented house, to come over to stay with me. He was with me until Madhura returned. Soon after, he married Rashmi, an officer in the Indian Administrative Service. She was due for posting in Delhi, and they settled down in their new quarters close by. Madhura and Rashmi became very good friends, especially after the Shroffs came over to Washington DC; they were there when we left.

Morarji Desai, who had been among the major aspirants for the prime ministership, resigned and Krishnamachari succeeded him as Finance Minister. Shastri made a few other changes in his Cabinet and it was only after all that was a meeting of the PC convened. This was held in the Prime Minister's office in Parliament House, a brief one at which Shastri wished to get acquainted with the members and the PC's principal officers. Dressed in a white *kurta* and *dhoti*, with a Gandhi cap and a Nehru jacket, he looked even shorter and frailer.

In his opening remarks, the Prime Minister desired to know whether the Third Plan had progressed as anticipated and if so, what the PC's perspective for the Fourth Plan was. Asoka Mehta said that an appraisal of Third Plan achievements would soon be ready and that a brief draft on the likely dimensions and strategy for the Fourth Plan period had been submitted to Nehru some time before his death. He also told Shastri of Nehru's instruction to work out further details in consultation with central ministries and state governments. When he had listened to all this, the Prime Minister thanked the members and said he would like to meet the full PC for a detailed discussion sometime later. He asked Asoka Mehta to complete a mid-term appraisal of developments since 1960-61 for that meeting. As we left, we were struck by the Prime Minister's utter simplicity in both manners and language. He was neither charismatic like Nehru nor did he overtly seek to exercise authority. How much he was to change later was not obvious at that stage. But it was clear that he had a mind of his own and would sooner or later become a leader in his chosen way. This was patent when he met the full PC some months later in Yojana Bhavan.

He started off by saying that things on the external front had worsened; the Chinese army had moved into Aksai Chin in the north and had advanced considerably in the middle and north-eastern sectors. The Chinese government had refused to recognise the McMahon line as the frontier between the two countries. Shastri continued that along the western and eastern borders, Pakistan had begun amassing troops and, given its alliance with the Chinese, could mount attacks any time. He saw no alternative to strengthening the defence forces as much as possible quickly. At the same time, he was keen that foodgrain production should be fully safeguarded, so that the rural population did not suffer or food prices rise. In these circumstances, he desired an early meeting of the National Development Council at which both the progress in the Third Plan as well as the principal development tasks for the Fourth Plan period could be defined. Meantime, he wished that the PC, in association with the ministries concerned and state governments, would examine the technical feasibility of some of the proposals put forward by it in its earlier draft of the Fourth Plan. New Delhi, which revelled in gossip, saw in these brief meetings with the PC signs of its reduced prestige and importance under the new premier.

When the National Development Council met a couple of months later, the state chief ministers decided to include themselves in the planning process by setting up several working groups consisting of central and state ministers together with members of the PC. Principal among these were working groups concerned with agriculture, saving and investment outlays and infrastructure development (especially irrigation, power and communications). While all this was going on, war broke out between India and Pakistan and work on the Fourth Plan was virtually suspended. Other developments such as reduced agricultural output in 1965-66 and interruption of foreign aid also intervened and domestic prices went up. However, despite his preoccupation with the war effort, the Prime Minister wished to meet the full PC before meeting a high-level Soviet delegation which was in Delhi for urgent discussions. At this meeting, he told the PC that the

Indian army had won a decisive tank battle on the western front and was about to move on to Lahore (in Pakistan). This was obviously good news, but he also said that he was very unhappy with the fall in food production and wanted the PC to take immediate steps to remedy the situation. With this instruction, he left, and the PC and the Agriculture Minister were to work out a strategy for raising food production quickly. This depended on increasing production per acre. It was also necessary to ensure that there was no hoarding of foodgrains by traders in anticipation of price rises. Applying himself to these tasks, the new agriculture minister, C Subramaniam, set about devising policies for more irrigation, development of better seeds, intensive application of chemical fertilisers, more agricultural credit and addition to agriculture extension services. He also set up the Food Corporation of India (FCI) to procure grains and arrange for an enlarged public distribution system. While all this was going on, Shastri left in January 1966 for Tashkent where the Soviet premier Kosygin had arranged a peace meeting between him and General Ayub Khan, the President of Pakistan. Peace was achieved but the Prime Minister did not return alive from Tashkent.

V

The death of two prime ministers in rapid succession naturally upset the country's economic and political environment. A hiatus developed in the making of economic policy. On the political front, the central government's power and authority suffered a setback, as who would head it remained uncertain. Within the ruling Congress Party, there were differences among leaders from the states. Apart from a common antipathy towards Morarji Desai, they could not agree on who should be their nominee for the premiership. Meanwhile, the ongoing hostilities with China and Pakistan had enlarged the Centre's non-development expenditure for defence purposes, limiting budgetary resources available for the Plan. Schemes and programmes included in the Third Plan were delayed and achievement under it was unsatisfactory. Gross public savings at current prices in 1964-65, which had risen to 3.3 per cent of GDP in 1964-66 fell to 2.3 per cent by 1966-67; two successive crop failures brought down the index for foodgrains output (1969-70=100) from 94.5 in 1964-65 to 77.1 in 1966-67.[1]

The new agriculture policies had yet to produce the "green revolution" and it was important to add to food availability through imports. This was not easy as the US and other countries had suspended military and development assistance when the India-Pakistan war broke out. In these circumstances, the PC was obliged to revise the draft Fourth Plan submitted earlier to Nehru. The National Development Council, which met a couple of months before Shastri's death, and the sub-committees set up by it had yet to produce their reports. However, as the first year of the Fourth Plan was to start on 1 April 1967, the PC was asked by the interim premier (Nanda) to ready the annual plan for 1967-68, which was to be woven into the Fourth Plan later.

After much confabulation within the Congress, Indira Gandhi was chosen to head the next government. She took charge in early February 1966 and among the first things she did was reconstitute the PC. Besides assuming the chairmanship and keeping Asoka Mehta as her deputy, she elevated Tarlok Singh to a full-time member. Among the ministerial members, she brought in the new Finance Minister, Sachindra Chaudhury, besides Nanda and Subramaniam. Indira Gandhi also strengthened the prime minister's office (PMO) substantially and proceeded to constitute a select group of ministers and other advisers to assist her. This came to be known pejoratively as her kitchen cabinet. Asoka Mehta was reportedly one of its members. She also decided to go to both the UK and the US to seek help in securing food and foreign aid. For this visit, my division quickly put together a brief for her on India's achievements since 1950-51, the urgency for food assistance, the basic thrust of the Plans and the extent of foreign assistance needed for development purposes.

While all this was going on, the World Bank had sent yet another mission under Bernard Bell to review the Indian economy's prospects and the kind of foreign aid it might require in future years. Two events probably prompted this second World Bank mission. First, the Soviet Union had begun discussions with the Government of India for increased military and development assistance when such aid from the West was suspended in 1965. Second, as a counterweight to the growing influence of China in South and South-East Asia, informed opinion in the US favoured resumption of aid to India. President Lyndon Johnson, who had succeeded the assassinated John F Kennedy, was particularly impressed by the advocacy of Walt Rostow and Max Milliken, both of Harvard, on behalf of India. External developments not only favoured a resumption but also an increase of aid to India.

However, 1966 was an exceedingly difficult year. Increased spending by the government for defence plus development, together with crop failures and reduced foreign exchange available for food or raw material imports, had pushed up domestic prices substantially despite a plethora of price and distribution controls. There was a flourishing black market and growing discontent with the regime of restrictions on market operations. The fiscal balance had been upset and the PC's efforts to maintain the tempo of industrial investment tended to be increasingly met with unwillingness, if not positive resistance, by state governments as well as central ministries. It was at this juncture that the Bell mission added its heavy criticism of government policies and programmes, besides arguing that the PC's obsession with the "big push" had resulted in neglect of investment in agriculture and quick-maturing programmes. The government had also ignored the export sector. The mission had gone on to say that the rupee needed to be devalued, both to encourage exports and limit imports. There were also other viewpoints which militated against government policies, such as investment in railways instead of road development, control of capital issues, resistance to technological development and so forth. Though the Bell mission dealt mainly with the Ministry of Finance, its views on investment structure, controls on domestic enterprises, fiscal rectitude and devaluation were all sensitive issues and the PC had no stomach for this open discussion. Bell quickly found that he was not entirely welcome in Yojana Bhavan.[2]

The MIT centre in New Delhi was, however, something else. In early 1965, its contacts with the PC were pretty close since both were interested in questions of medium to long-term economic development. One of its mentors in Harvard at that time was Rosenstein Rodan, the originator of the "big push" theory of concentrated investment for structural change. The Harvard outfit also believed (presumably) that India was at a "take-off" stage and required massive assistance to see it through. And conveniently for Pitambar Pant and me, the Delhi outfit of the centre had some talented economists fully conversant with operational research who could be of assistance in our input-output analysis. Both the perspective planning division and my division had research personnel who could work with the MIT centre's specialists in processing masses of data at the computer facility of the IIT in Kanpur. We therefore had been working closely with the MIT centre, leaving aside many of the sensitive issues relevant in the short period. In particular, we could do our projections on the assumption of constant (rupee or dollar) prices. Though not completely but for the most part, we could keep the purely monetary and fiscal issues on one side. My intention at that stage was to weave these later into whatever projections we had jointly developed with the MIT centre.

This working relationship ended abruptly in late 1965, when it became widely known in Delhi that the MIT centre in Harvard was partly financed by the US government's Central Intelligence Agency (CIA), and that Millikan (who had been mainly responsible for founding the Delhi centre) was once its employee. This revelation gathered greater weight when the PC's deputy chairman Asoka Mehta received a letter from Ambassador B K Nehru in Washington DC about his visit to the MIT in Harvard. In that letter, he stressed the need to alter the investment pattern of the Fourth Plan to ensure higher production of foodgrains and other consumer articles. Earlier in 1965, Subramaniam had also been advised by President Johnson that India should enlarge her food supply and not depend on US food aid. In conjunction with the revelation of the CIA-MIT Centre connection, this completely altered the environment for our collaboration. We perceived in this an attempt on the part of the US government to influence India's decision on development strategy which, in any case, it was trying to push through the World Bank. The PC came to believe that many of the Bell mission recommendations, including in particular the necessity of devaluing the Indian rupee, were inspired by the US via its executive directors on the Fund and the World Bank. Further efforts by some senior members of the MIT centre, such as Rodan and Millikan only made things worse. Both divisions – Pitambar Pant's and mine – ceased further collaboration with the Delhi centre, which was soon closed.

When all this was happening, I was invited by the president of the World Bank, George Woods, to go to Washington DC as director of the EDI for five years beginning April 1967. Since the Fourth Plan had been put in cold storage, I sought Asoka Mehta's permission to accept this offer. As I had come to the PC on deputation from the RBI, I also said that its concurrence was required. He agreed to let me go and wrote to the RBI for extension of my deputation, to which the Bank agreed somewhat reluctantly. I wrote back to Woods that I would be in the EDI around April 1967.

Meanwhile, there was a new development. Whether it was due to leakage of the Bell mission's proposal or the IMF's references to an overvalued rupee hampering exports, Delhi's rumour mill was abuzz with talk of devaluation being made a condition for provision of foreign aid by the consortium. Apparently, some behind-the-scene discussions were going on between New Delhi, the RBI, the IMF and the World Bank. Whether linking Plan assistance to devaluation and other policy changes was indicated to Indira Gandhi during her Washington visit was not clear. However, soon after her return, Finance Minister Krishnamachari, who did not favour any change in the rupee's par value, resigned and was succeeded by Chaudhury. Speculatation about the imminence of devaluation gathered momentum. The PC's decision to prepare the annual plan for 1966-67 and postpone work on the Fourth Plan added further grist to the rumour mill. When I met Asoka Mehta, I told him that there was much talk in New Delhi about devaluation of the rupee being a condition for more aid from the World Bank. I also said I saw no benefit in devaluation as our exports were neither price nor income elastic, while imports, mostly for projects, would become more expensive. Further the rupee counterparts of our foreign debt repayments would affect the government's budget adversely. He nodded but said nothing – which should have been an indication to me of his position.

VI

Things moved fast after that. When Asoka Mehta was later asked to head a mission to Washington DC for the ostensible purpose of securing more aid from the World Bank, it was all too clear that something major was afoot. He asked me to go with him on that mission saying that the main objective was to secure a substantial World Bank loan. I found that apart from me, the mission consisted of two senior officers of the Finance Ministry, which should have alerted me to the possibility of other issues coming up, including discussions with the IMF. A couple of days later, I was summoned to an urgent meeting in the Prime Minister's house late in the evening. Apart from Asoka Mehta and Subrahmaniam, the meeting included L K Jha, the Prime Minister's Principal Secretary; P C Bhattacharya, Governor of the RBI; I G Patel, Economic Affairs Secretary in the Finance Ministry; P Govindan Nair, Additional Secretary in the same Ministry; and V K Ramaswami, Economic Adviser in that Ministry. When the meeting began, Ramaswami and I were asked to wait in the next chamber. It was perhaps an hour later that we were called in for discussing the aid India should seek from the World Bank. Whether by then Ramaswami was aware of the government's intention to devalue the rupee, I was not sure. As we went in, the issue being considered was the size and form of external aid we should seek for the next few years. Asoka Mehta asked me to detail the assistance we needed for the Plan from the World Bank; Ramaswami then explained the position regarding the balance of payments situation and what sort of short-term credits India could seek from the IMF. After we both had our say, the Prime Minister concluded the meeting, saying she would convey the gist of the meeting to the Cabinet, which was to meet the next day, and that we should be ready to leave for Washington DC immediately.

The four of us (Asoka Mehta, Govindan Nair, Ramaswami and I) reached Palam airport for the Air-India flight that night and were led into the lounge. While other formalities were being completed, Govindan Nair came over to have a word with me. It was then that I learnt that he and Ramaswami would discuss the issue of rupee devaluation with the Fund, while I was to go with Asoka Mehta for meetings at the Bank. This was shocking news to me. I resented having been left out of discussions on this vital matter and told Govindan Nair so; and before we left, I told Asoka Mehta that there was little point in accepting such conditional assistance. Such a move would have serious economic and political repercussions, and make nonsense of all our projections on the basis of constant prices. I made it clear to him that I was not in favour of any change in the exchange value of the rupee and also that he should not ask me to go with him since he did not have full confidence in me on such a major question of policy. All that he said was that I should not leave at that late stage in the interest of the government and the need for secrecy. Perhaps I should have had the courage to walk out at that point, even if it meant returning to the RBI. Since the governor of the RBI was also a party to the decision at the Prime Minister's meeting, exiting at that stage would have probably meant quitting the RBI as well. I just did not have the courage to say "so be it," a decision which has shamed me no end.

What transpired at the mission's meetings in Washington DC has now become part of history. There were actually two separate meetings – one with the IMF in which Govindan Nair and Ramaswami participated; and the other with Ramaswami and me with the then economic adviser to the World Bank, Irving Freidman. The substance of both these meetings was reported to Asoka Mehta after dinner each night. In these meetings, either the executive director for India on the Fund or the Bank as the case may be, or his alternate, took part. It soon became obvious that the IMF and the World Bank had already agreed on "conditional support" – some specified amount of foreign exchange assistance to India on the condition that it agreed to a measure of currency devaluation and other policies. This had very likely been conveyed to Asoka Mehta during his private meetings with the managing director of the Fund and the president of the World Bank. It was not clear how much they had been influenced by the report of the Bell mission or by discussions in their respective executive boards. Whatever the reason, it was soon clear from our discussions that the Bank's assistance was contingent on the Fund's acceptance of rupee devaluation of a certain order. Details on this matter – by how much or in what stages – would be decided by the Fund. The Bank would consider the extent and nature of its assistance, beyond what India would be entitled to draw as credit from the Fund.

As the mission's discussions progressed, it became abundantly clear that this matter of a realignment of the rupee's par value had been an issue ever since Woods, a former New York banker had succeeded Eugene Black as the World Bank's president, at about the same time as Pierre-Paul Schweitzer had become the IMF's managing director. In the PC we were familiar with the change in the Bank, and with Woods' predilections – which were all free-market oriented and anti-public sector. We did not have any continuing contact with the Fund. This was one of the reasons for me to keep out of discussions with the Fund; I had no idea what had gone on between the Fund, Finance Ministry and the RBI, which handled foreign exchange resources. However, since 1963-64, those of us in the PC who had participated in the Third Plan's mid-term appraisal were aware of changes in economic conditions which, sooner or later, were likely to bring the IMF into policy discussions with the government. Since March 1963, domestic inflation had been gaining strength, with the wholesale price index going up from 110.2 in March 1963 to 149.9 in March 1966 and 167.3 in March 1967. The rise in food prices was even steeper, from 115.4 in March 1963 to 171.1 in March 1966 and further to 207.8 by March 1967 (1961-62=100 in both cases). Foreign exchange reserves (including gold and foreign assets of the RBI, government balances abroad and net borrowings from the IMF) had come down to the equivalent of Rs 237 crore by December 1964, which would hardly cover imports for a couple of months. These elementary indications of impending balance of payments (and par value) problems had been the main theme of the Bell report. That report had proceeded to argue that the combination of price inflation and foreign exchange stringency had arisen largely from Plan expenditure, which involved both domestic and foreign expenditure, in excess of what the economy could bear. Bell wanted an increase in "market flexibilities" – which was his shorthand for a bonfire of price, distribution and import controls together with the encouragement of exports. It was in the latter context that he wanted the rupee's par value to be adjusted. Much of this was disclosed to me in meetings with Freidman. But apparently it was not news to Ramaswami or Govindan Nair, who were aware of their Ministry's discussions with the Fund. The only issue on the foreign aid requirements of the Third Plan and beyond which Freidman raised was that it should be reassessed to ensure that current needs of the agricultural and industrial sectors were met fully through "maintenance imports" and project imports managed on the basis of whatever consortium assistance was specifically so provided.

It was a disappointing mission for me for more reasons than one. Though there had been ample discussion in India on the pros and cons of policy changes – including devaluation and decontrol – I had not been a party to all the discussions that Asoka Mehta was having with the Finance Ministry, much less the PMO. That the decision to devalue had been decided even before we left was disclosed to me at the very last minute. As head of the mission, Asoka Mehta gave no indication of what issues had come up during his discussions with Woods, Schweitzer, Ambassador Nehru or Anjaria (then India's executive director on the Fund). It was during our meetings with Freidman that Ramaswami gave indications that India was willing to consider devaluation if adequate aid was forthcoming. At the PC, we had assessed our requirements for Plan purposes which would be $1billion a year. The bulk of this was for projects, both infrastructural and industrial. We had also provided for some imports of industrial raw materials, fertilisers, foodgrains, and so on, or, in the Commission's parlance, "maintenance imports". In the PC, we believed that by the end of the Fourth Plan, the nation's industrial sector would be able to produce enough machinery and spares to reduce the need for project imports.

This aspect of import substitution was not palatable to the aid-givers, who hoped that as India's GDP rose, its import bill would also grow. It was to finance imports in a larger measure that the Bell mission had argued for lifting of controls on imports, prices and distribution. Our contention was that most of our exports consisted of agricultural commodities, which were not particularly price elastic. Even if they were so, there would be the problem of supply inelasticities, given the country's food requirements, man-land ratio, agricultural conditions and so forth. The case for devaluation was in my view not a strong one, and that it was being forced on us by Washington left me very unhappy.

When we flew out of Delhi, I had no idea that the Prime Minister had approved of devaluation and discussion with the Fund was only about the extent of change in the rupee's par value. Mehta and I left Washington without any commitment by the World Bank on provision of additional aid, and without any knowledge on my part of what else had actually been decided. On the way back, we touched London, where P N Haksar, the Deputy High Commissioner for India, took me aside and asked me what exactly the World Bank had promised. At that point, I had nothing more to say than that it would seriously consider what aid to give and in what form. Haksar was very upset and must have assumed that I did not want to share with him the details of the agreement with the Fund and the Bank. He told me that the UK government was full of talk about rupee devaluation and he was not prepared to accept that I did not know the details. He reminded me of this later, much to my chagrin when I met him some years later as deputy chairman of the PC. My position as part of what has since come to be known as the devaluation mission was also compromised by my having accepted a couple of months earlier the World Bank's invitation to join as director of the EDI. During the Asoka Mehta mission, I was invited by Woods for a lunch meeting at which John Adler, the director of the EDI, and Richard Demuth, member of the president's inner council, were present. The timing of this was unfortunate as it became widely known that I would be taking over from Adler in April 1967. It was hard to convince people that there was no connection between the mission and the job offer and that I had accepted the World Bank offer months earlier. Both Pitambar Pant and I G Patel were upset that Asoka Mehta had agreed and even prevailed upon the RBI to let me go directly from Delhi to Washington DC.

Leaving that aside, devaluation was not something that the Congress Party expected the new Prime Minister to accept so soon after her elevation and there was strong disagreement among its leaders. Likewise, several prominent economists (including Rao and Raj) did not consider devaluation a wise move. They felt that a change in the rupee's par value was unlikely to benefit the balance of payments, much less domestic prices. Apart from making project imports dearer in rupee terms, it would not be conducive to dampening domestic inflation, which, due to a severe drought, had already pushed up food prices. Altogether, they did not believe that the post-devaluation period would witness the classical template of consequences.

Indira Gandhi's decision was not a popular one. When it became clear in the subsequent months that the promised assistance of $1 billion per year for three years was not forthcoming, the Asoka Mehta mission was blamed for selling "the country's honour" for nothing in return. I was not in Delhi when the decision to devalue the rupee by 36.5 per cent was announced. When some time later I returned to Yojana Bhavan, it was by no means a warm reception that awaited me. Neither the PC members nor the senior officers believed that I had not been a privy to the government's decision. It was not easy to live in Delhi with that kind of notoriety.

Everything went haywire in the PC after that. As inflation worsened in the subsequent months, no decision would be taken on the Fourth Plan. Instead, a succession of annual plans followed for the next three years. Asoka Mehta left the PC as did Rao. Pitambar Pant was very unhappy that Indira Gandhi, whom he had known for many years, had kept him in the dark until after the announcement. My relations with various ministries which had been taken by surprise worsened. Since work on the Fourth Plan had given way to a series of annual plans – which depended mostly on what the Finance Ministry provided in annual budgets – there was hardly any scope left for developing even a medium-term perspective. The PC ceased to be the exciting place it was when I joined it. I was not unhappy to get out of New Delhi at that stage.

VII

We reached Washington DC towards the end of April 1967 and found that as before the World Bank had booked us at the Dupont Plaza hotel. Raj, who was visiting the EDI as guest faculty for a year, and his family were also in the same hotel, which was a bonus for us. Since we could stay there for a month before moving out, we had ample time to get used to the city.

I went the next morning to the World Bank and was happy to meet several friends who had stayed on, such as Badri Rao and his wife Saroja. The bank had grown in size and occupied the entire building on 1818, H Street NW. The IMF had moved across 19th Street NW to a new building; so had the EDI to a building on G Street NW, behind the bank. I walked over there to meet my old friend Adler, the institute's director, who took me round to meet others in the EDI and in the Bank. I also met my own friends like P S Narayana Prasad, India's executive director on the Fund, and S Jagannathan, his counterpart on the Bank's board. They both knew me from my earlier years in the RBI and the PC.

In the preceding years, the EDI had added some project courses to its basic programme on macroeconomic development. These new courses, focusing on project identification, evaluation and policy were offered in French and Spanish besides English.

A similar course on education was to be offered later. As before, course outlines and selected reading had to be provided to the participants. With more courses and more participants, the World Bank had acquired an apartment building near the EDI to house the participants. To familiarise the participants with the specific problems of developing economies, guest faculty from them were invited each year. During my tenure, professors Raj and Minhas from India, Aboyade from Nigeria and Javier Marquez from Mexico assisted us.

Before I took over, the EDI had experimented with national programmes conducted outside Washington DC in association with reputed local institutions, mostly in Iran and India. Based on that experience, we decided to have more regional programmes outside – jointly with local institutions. The intention was that after this initial effort, the local partner would be encouraged to offer more such courses, with some financial and academic support from the EDI. These joint programmes were later extended to the French and Spanish-speaking regions of Africa and South America. For use in these programmes, reading materials were prepared at the EDI and distributed widely. To identify appropriate institutions to host these joint programmes, I toured the English-speaking countries of Asia and Africa while my colleagues covered the French and Spanish-speaking nations. In addition, those in Washington courses were taken on educational tours to Spain, Mexico, Colombia, Brazil and Jamaica. All this involved much travel for me and others in the EDI.

As a member of the World Bank's economic and loan committees I had to attend them as well as the Executive Board meetings and the Bank-Fund annual conferences. In both the committees there would be extensive discussion of the borrowing country's capability to execute bank-financed projects as well as its repayment capability. When Woods was president, he did not favour government-sponsored projects, though borrowing governments had to be guarantors of bank-financed private projects. His focus tended to be on repayment schedules, the project's internal rate of return and such details. It was not until Robert McNamara took over as president that both the World Bank and the EDI could take up social service programmes, sector policies and broader entities for either financing or study. He made more extensive use of the IDA's resources for long-gestation and local finance projects.

Though McNamara recognised the need for financing social service sectors, his approach was basically market-oriented and he was not really fond of the EDI's involvement in national development courses. This changed somewhat after his tour of Asian developing countries, including India and Pakistan. He recognised the need for governments to spend extensively on education and public health programmes, as well as on administrative improvements. Even so, his attitude towards the EDI continued to be dominated by a preference for project courses. By 1970, my interest in the EDI diminished sufficiently to make me want to return to India. Prime Minister Indira Gandhi came at that time to Washington, as East Pakistan agitated to become independent of West Pakistan. Relations between India and the US became tense as India-Pakistan relations worsened. Indira Gandhi's meeting with President Richard Nixon did not go well and she decided to express herself freely during a public address in the Washington Cathedral. We were there, listening to her powerful speech, which enhanced our desire to go back home. My mother's death in 1971 further strengthened the wish to return by end of that year. McNamara asked me to stay on as an adviser in the Bank's economic department but my heart was no longer there and I declined the offer so that I could get back for more meaningful work in India.

All this apart, our Washington years were momentous ones for both the US and India. Heavy losses in Vietnam and an effective media blitz led the US to withdraw its troops from South-East Asia, with considerable ignominy. There were in those years a great Afro-American march to Washington DC; and the assassinations of Martin Luther King Jr and Robert Kennedy, the prospective Democratic contestant for the US presidency. McNamara had to move out of defence and, as mentioned earlier, was shifted to the World Bank. US pride was somewhat restored by the successful landing of its astronauts on the moon. This achievement was soon clouded by the Watergate scandal, resulting later in Nixon's resignation. By then Afro-Americans had won the right to become full and equal citizens of the US.

The bonus for us from our second tour of the EDI was the joy of meeting old friends and making new ones, both American and

Indian. Several of them continue to give us pleasure even now. My travels on behalf of the EDI had added to my list of friends in other countries as well. All told we were glad to have spent those years in Washington DC. My return to the RBI turned out to be well-timed. By the time my wife and children joined me, I had been allotted a flat by the Bank, which was a major benefit; we did not have to go searching for a house.

NOTES

1 EPWRF: *National Accounts Statistics 1950-51 to 2000-01,* p 30; RBI: *Chart Book on Financial and National Indicators,* Tables 8.2 and 8.6.

2 The Bell mission's meetings with government officials became progressively less cordial. When Mr. Bell said that he spoke with the authority of Bank president, Dr. I.G. Patel told him severely that he spoke with the authority of the Indian Government and closed the meeting.

7

The Difficult Years

I

S JAGANNATHAN, who was India's executive director on the World Bank's board, had taken over as governor of the RBI in late 1968, and I joined as principal adviser on economic issues in 1972. By then Ravi Hazari had moved in as deputy governor, after a short stint as editor of the *EPW*. There had been many changes in the government, indicating a major extension of the authority of Prime Minister Indira Gandhi. After the split in the Congress Party in 1969, Indira Gandhi had prevailed on the Communist Party of India (CPI) to support her government and proceeded to nationalise 14 of India's principal private banks.[1] Privy purses and the privileges of former princes whose states had merged with the Indian Union were abolished and many controls and stipulations imposed on businesses and commodity markets, in pursuance of resource allocation as well as socialist equity. The power of the PMO under Haksar had grown while that of individual ministries declined. The PC had been reconstituted, with D R Gadgil as Chairman and several new members. There were already indications of growing labour troubles, especially in railways, ports and other public enterprises.

The big change that had occurred before my return to India was the emergence of Bangladesh as a fully independent country. In that country's struggle for independence from Pakistan, India had provided some assistance, including military help. When popular uprisings in East Pakistan became intense, and Indian troops had been strengthened along the eastern border, Pakistan attacked India along the western border, only to be repulsed with heavy losses. Indira Gandhi exhibited great resolve and strength at that juncture, making it clear to both China and the US, staunch allies of Pakistan, that any move on their part to assist the aggressor would be resisted resolutely. The country rallied behind her as never before and military engagements along both the eastern and western borders succeeded triumphantly. Indira Gandhi's stock in India as well as outside rose sharply, and Pakistan sued for peace along with accepting the independence of Bangladesh. By the time I returned to India in 1972, South Asia's map had changed considerably, in some ways to India's advantage.

However, war expenses and other related policy changes had not been accompanied by robust changes on the economic front. The foodgrain index of production which had gone up to nearly 113 in 1970-71 (base triennium ending 1969-70=100) came down to 102 two years later and languished there for some time. The famed green revolution had benefited the wheat crop but not rice or coarse grains production, and when, with the outbreak of the Bangladesh war, foreign aid inflows stopped, the availability of wheat in fair price shops diminished. Consequently, the food prices index which was around 196.8 in 1969-70 (1961-62=100) went up sharply to 210.3 in 1971-72 and further to 295.6 a couple of years later. As always, money wages had not moved up commensurately and labour unions became restive.

In this situation, Indira Gandhi decided on general elections in 1971 on the promise of *garibi hatao* (abolish poverty), which probably gave her considerable political advantage. But it also intensified the agitation for higher wages by labour, supported in many instances by organisations professing ideologies different from that of the Congress Party. Both the Jana Sangh, a professedly "Hindu" organisation, and the Left parties supported these agitations in their separate ways, and, in general, there was growing evidence of economic and social unrest all over the country.

Some of these dissatisfactions and tensions had also crept into the RBI. With the policy of "social control" of commercial banks introduced by Morarji Desai in 1967, the RBI's exclusive authority on private banks was to some extent reduced by government prescriptions on priorities in granting credit facilities. But the major change was with the promulgation of the Banking Companies (Acquisition and Transfer of Undertakings) Ordinance 1969, under which major banks had been nationalised. The government became the owner of these banks and to ensure that they operated in accordance with its instructions, a new Department of Banking had been set up in the Finance Ministry. The responsibility for appointing the chairmen and managing directors (CMDs) of public-sector banks, and nominating the members of banks' boards of directors, was taken over by the government. Though the RBI was technically empowered to issue instructions to individual banks, it was inevitable that banks' CMDs would check with the Department of Banking for concurrence. However, the RBI continued to be the authority for licensing bank branches, credit authorisation, periodic inspection, specification of performance criteria, interest rates, and so forth – in other words, the details of control and supervision of banking operations in the country. But on broad matters of policy affecting credit creation and use, interference by the government increased from year to year. It did not help that most governors of the RBI – and also some deputy governors – belonged to the Indian Administrative Service, with a natural tendency to maintain good relations with those in power. By the 1970s, relations between the RBI and the central government had changed enough to deny the former much of the prestige and independence it should have had as arbiter of the country's monetary policy.

The result was that as the Bank's principal economic adviser, I had to often second guess what the government's reaction would be before advising the management on any change of RBI policy. This was not always easy, until it became clear that decision-making in the government had shifted substantially to the PMO and Indira Gandhi's close advisers. For some years after I rejoined the RBI, Hazari enjoyed good relations with the PMO. This did not last long; but while it lasted, it caused problems between him and the governor. Having known him well for many years, I had a good rapport with him and our relations were free and informal. He often walked over to my room for serious discussions or just gossip over tea, and this was known widely enough in the Bank for others trying to find out what we had discussed. That apart, both of us had to visit New Delhi frequently for discussions with the Finance Minister. On such occasions, I found it useful to go across to the PMO and check with some of my friends there what was cooking. Like all other public institutions, the RBI management also had to maintain good relations with the PMO.

II

With the nationalisation of commercial banks, together with RBI ownership of the SBI and its associate banks in different states, the Bank had become heavily involved in licensing new bank branches, enunciating priorities in credit policy, lead bank programmes, scrutiny and authorisation of credits over a specified amount (known commonly as the credit authorisation scheme or CAS), periodic inspection of banks, processing of banking returns, and so on. As principal adviser, I was concerned only with the broader policy questions to do with patterns of banks' expansion and credit structure, apart from those of monetary management. There were frequent discussions with the Department of Banking and the Ministry of Finance on detailed aspects of branch licensing with which neither I nor the economic department was concerned. These were handled by the department of banking operations and development (DBOD), which was under Hazari. However, there were enough issues related to the general economy and policies for ensuring adequate credit availability for development without exacerbating inflationary pressures or balance of payments problems with which my department was mainly concerned. It was also my responsibility to promote medium- or long-term research in the economic department, on the basis of primary data flowing into the DBOD, agricultural credit, and exchange control departments. Much of this later went into the *RBI Monthly Bulletin*, the *Annual Report, Report on Currency and Finance, Trends and Progress of Banking*, and so on. The areas of research on monetary and banking affairs were sometimes thrown up in inter-departmental discussions. For the most part, however, it was left to the directors of each division of the economic department to work out its annual research programme – subject, as always, to the time and personnel that could be spared after preparing such memoranda as the Bank's management might want. The department's involvement in banking affairs had increased significantly after the nationalisation of commercial banks. Additionally, two other developments which had occurred while I was away had also involved the economic department. In the mid-1960s, the government had decided to constitute two separate institutions under the RBI to look after the long-term needs of the agricultural sector – the Agricultural Refinance and Development Corporation (ARDC) – and of major industries – the IDBI. Each was to be looked after by a deputy governor of the RBI and was in the process of building up its separate wings of economists and statisticians. But in 1972, they were drawing heavily on the Bank's economics and statistics departments. Within a couple of years, several senior officers in my department were transferred to these two organisations. There was also a third institution to assist the industrial sector, the Unit Trust of India (UTI), which was to be helped by the RBI. However, not long after, these institutions were made directly answerable to the government, with only a tenuous link to the Bank. Over the years, they organised their own advisory departments, and the RBI came into the picture only when their activities impinged on commercial bank operations or on the broader questions of inflation, interest rates or balance of payments.

A couple of years later, I was appointed as an executive director (ED) of the RBI. This enlarged my responsibilities and besides the economics and statistics departments, the credit planning cell (CPC) came under me and increased my involvement with credit policy. Hazari also proceeded to have me share some of the tasks of the DBOD, especially the CAS and credit priorities. As an ED, I was required to attend the governor's weekly meetings with deputy governors, as well as those of the committee of the central board. After the nationalisation of banks, the Finance Minister had started periodic regional meetings with the banks concerned, to supervise the extent to which the credit requirements in each state, especially in rural areas, were met. These regional meetings were primarily intended to promote closer cooperation between the field officers of state governments and branch managements of banks. More often than not, there were more complaints in these meetings than mutual appreciation of each other's efforts to help rural borrowers.

Alongside these changes in domestic banking, the international financial situation was changing rapidly for the worse. In August 1971, the US government suspended free convertibility of the dollar into gold at the long-standing rate of $35 per ounce. Though India maintained its rupee value of the US dollar at Rs 7.50, the dollar's going off gold virtually ended the IMF's system of par values. Several European currencies had begun to float and the dollar-sterling cross-rate varied from day to day. In consequence, though the rupee-dollar exchange rate had not changed, considerable confusion about the sanctity of par values prevailed. V G Pendharkar (at that time an ED of the Bank) dealt with this matter directly and I had only to keep track of variations that occurred from time to time in the rupee-sterling-dollar-Special

Drawing Rights (SDR) nexus. But when Pendharkar left and I took over as an ED, my involvement with exchange rate policies increased. Though the RBI had decided to keep the rupee-dollar cross-rate unchanged when the latter went off gold, questions remained on what to do with other trading currencies, especially the pound sterling. For the next few years, this remained a matter of concern to both the government and the RBI.

Before becoming fully involved with the DBOD, I was asked by the government to head a committee to report on the availability and pricing of crude oil and petroleum products. This required my having to visit crude oil-producing areas as well as oil refineries in India to collect detailed information on the processes involved, costs and factory prices, as well as to hold discussions with those engaged in retailing the end products. Until then, crude oil pricing was on an import parity basis, as most of it was imported. But as more crude became available from domestic wells, we decided to recommend adoption of the marginal social cost principle for domestic crude and work out an appropriate "pool" price for delivery of crude oil to refineries. We also suggested joint pricing of refinery products, using the product shares as weights. Following a couple of interim reports on this gamut of prices, and refinery and trade margins, the committee's final report was submitted in 1976.

It was during one of this committee's visits to New Delhi that I met Manmohan Singh, who was to become Prime Minister in 2004. He was then economic adviser to the Commerce Ministry. After a brilliant academic career in the UK and a spell at the United Nations Committee on Trade and Development (UNCTAD), he had returned to India for short stints in academia before joining the government. He held important positions in the Finance Ministry, was governor of the RBI and deputy chairman of the PC before becoming Finance Minister in 1991. Manmohan Singh and his wife Gursharan have been good friends to us ever since, regardless of the exalted position he occupies now.

There were enough issues connected with domestic policy to keep me busy. As ED, I shared with Hazari the responsibility for the DBOD as well as the CPC. Since each bank loan in excess of Rs 1 crore had to be authorised by the RBI, disputes on working capital requirements of traders or producers were frequent. For defining acceptable criteria, the RBI had appointed a committee under P L Tandon, consisting of both bankers and corporate borrowers. This committee included essential stocks of raw materials and finished goods together with "work-in-progress" in working capital needs. However, in reality, delays in customs clearance of imported raw materials or in domestic transit varied the duration of stocks from commodity to commodity. It was on this matter that disputes between the DBOD and banks or borrowers arose. Taking this into account, the committee had sought to prevent undue recourse to bank credit to finance stocks.

Working capital needs of industries and commerce were usually provided by banks under their cash-credit facility. This consisted of an upper limit to withdrawals by the client, within which credit based on the pledge of stocks was to be used, subject to a "margin". This allowed the customer to vary his stocks as necessary, depending on seasonal factors with respect to agricultural raw materials or transit delays in the case of domestic or imported industrial raw materials. Technically, such stocks were to be maintained in locked warehouses, the keys to which would be deposited with the bank concerned. Under the CAS, specific instructions had to be issued to the borrowers on periodic or occasional drawals from the stock. Altogether, the DBOD had to check a variety of issues before authorising the credit. This was a time-consuming process and the banks or customers often complained to the RBI about delays in authorisation. It was basically a cumbersome system. But it had been instituted as the RBI was keen on economising on bank credit for working capital purposes.

III

The 1970s turned out to be difficult years for the country. Apart from changes in the international system of par values resulting in floating exchange rates of some currencies, prices of crude oil went up steeply in October 1973. Domestically, Indira Gandhi had come back to power after the general election in 1971 and set about implementing the *garibi hatao* programme promised in her party's election manifesto. In pursuance of this policy, the PC was instructed to focus on employment creation through larger public investment. Both direct taxes and excise or customs duties on commodities considered as luxuries were stepped up. Despite these increases, budget deficits increased rapidly and the government borrowed heavily from the RBI. This in turn led to a tightening of the RBI's credit policy after 1971. The Bank rate and the statutory liquidity ratio (SLR) were raised progressively; by mid-1974, the Bank rate had gone up to 9 per cent and SLR to 33 per cent of total deposits. Interest on RBI refinance to banks went up gradually to a maximum of 18 per cent. This combination of high taxation and high interest rates adversely affected both domestic output and employment. Together with increased prices of petroleum products, internal economic conditions had become almost explosive.

The equivalent of a fuse was lit by the Allahabad High Court decision of June 1975 annulling Indira Gandhi's election to Parliament in 1971. This had been challenged by one of her election opponents on a variety of charges, from corruption to misuse of government facilities. It was in fact the last named minor misdemeanour which the presiding judge chose to consider illegal. It was of course open to Indira Gandhi to go to the Supreme Court on appeal; but she chose instead to declare an Emergency and assume absolute authority. India woke up on the morning of 26 June 1975 to find that an ordinance had empowered Indira Gandhi to function as the de facto ruler of India – not only the ultimate but sole authority.

The annulment of her election was like the straw that broke the camel's back. All of 1974 had witnessed a series of protests and demonstrations by workers, students and an assortment of political parties against the corruption and high-handedness of Indira Gandhi's government. Her ministers and officers indulged widely in "marketing" favours – licences, promotions, special concessions, foreign junkets and so on. Power had been systematically centralised and even the Supreme Court was packed with "committed" judges. Together with high prices and increasing venality in government at both the central and state levels, non-Congress parties of varying persuasions had become restive. The transport system was paralysed by a railway strike, the workers demanding higher wages to compensate for the price rise and better working conditions. Student movements in Gujarat and Bihar targeted the extensive corruption in their states and were met by police action. At this juncture, largely in support of the student movements, veteran leader Jayaprakash Narayan (JP) took up the fight to restore moral values in the country's administration, in political parties as well as business affairs – in fact in all aspects of the social and political life of the nation. The JP movement spread rapidly from state to state; and before long Indira Gandhi's government was faced with a nationwide opposition in which students, organised labour, farmers, NGOs of many kinds and social workers participated – some for better living conditions, others for values of importance to life. These circumstances, together with the decision of the Allahabad High Court, led Indira Gandhi to take the extreme step of declaring the Emergency and assuming total authority, virtually suspending the Constitution and rendering all branches of governance fully subservient to her.

Indira Gandhi's main contention against the JP movement was that it had become destructive of the bases of a democratic policy – violent, undisciplined, injurious to people and property and harmful to the "unity and integrity" of India. She promptly put the leaders concerned in jail, on grounds varying from disturbing the peace to indulging in black-marketing. JP, Morarji Desai, leaders of the Jana Sangh, communists and socialists, all found themselves behind bars for varying periods. Besides her intolerance of political opposition, she subjected all public institutions to straitjackets of more or less severity. Regardless of their political status, chief ministers of states were subordinated to her command. The central legislature was practically defunct, courts and the police had become subservient, and the administration was totally dependent on the orders of Indira Gandhi, her son Sanjay Gandhi and his cronies. An air of uncertainly prevailed over the country, unsure of what the government would do next or what the popular response would be.

The RBI and the nationalised commercial banks did not escape her attention for long. When the Allahabad Court decision came, I was in Paris, as part of a delegation led by Finance Minister Subramaniam. He was asked to return immediately to India, leaving behind a truncated mission of officials to report on subsequent discussions. Soon after the Finance Minister's return, the Emergency was declared. Indira Gandhi asked him to ensure that her programme for quicker development of branches in rural areas be taken up by public-sector banks. K R Puri, who was until then the chairman of the LIC, was appointed governor of the RBI, and J C Luther, an officer from the audit and accounts service, was deputed to the RBI as an ED with particular responsibility for commercial banking and foreign exchange operations. Both Puri and Luther were, according to the Delhi grapevine, close to Sanjay Gandhi and had been sent to the RBI at his instance. That apart, for Hazari and me, who until then were in sole charge of the DBOD, the CPC and the CAS, this was a clear indication that the banking industry was set to become yet another handmaiden of the political bosses.

The politicisation of banking had really started with the nationalisation of commercial banks in 1969. Since the RBI was the licensing authority, issues connected with branch expansion figured in many Parliament questions, which had to be answered through the Ministry of Finance. Partly because of the concentration of commercial banks' main offices in Bombay, Calcutta, Madras and Delhi, more branches were opened in the initial years in the western, southern and northern states. It was the RBI's policy to ensure a 3:1 ratio between rural and urban (and metropolitan) branches. Licences had been issued by the RBI all over India on this basis, but progress was more rapid in the western and southern states than in Uttar Pradesh, Madhya Pradesh, Rajasthan, Bihar, Orissa or the North-Eastern states, resulting in an uneven distribution of rural branches. State governments and members of Parliament often complained of preferential treatment by the RBI of commercially advanced states and neglect of those which badly needed more bank branches. Another major complaint was that where rural branches had been set up, their deposit-credit ratios were not commensurate with the requirements of organised credit by agriculture and rural industries. The complaint in effect was that banks were systematically denying credit facilities to farmers in dire need but transferring rural savings to urban investments. Many such questions – including denial of bank credit to specific individuals or categories of farmers – were raised in regional conferences of banks which were chaired by the Finance Minister, with the chief ministers of the states concerned, the governor and his deputy dealing with the DBOD, CMDs of principal banks and senior officers of the central and state governments in attendance. Progressively, the chairmen of public-sector banks tended to seek the approval of the Department of Banking in Delhi rather than the RBI in Bombay until later, under Indira Gandhi in the 1980s, the politicisation of public sector banks became complete.

Since nationalisation had made the Government of India the sole owner of public-sector banks, the CMDs of these banks as well as their executive directors and boards had become government appointees. Their terms and conditions of service were determined by the Department of Banking. On each bank's board, there was a nominee of the Finance Ministry, without whose approval no transaction was possible. There was, of course, also a nominee of the RBI, but his main concern was only to see that directives issued with regard to cash reserves, statutory liquidity, interest rates, priority ratios, performance criteria and so on were observed. Though the SBI was owned by the RBI, its chairman and managing director were appointed from the beginning by the Finance Ministry, largely from the Indian Administrative Service. However, as the majority owner of its equity, the RBI director on the SBI's board remained a potent factor, probably because one of the deputy governors represented it.

Matters came to a head on the opening of foreign branches by Indian banks, especially public-sector banks. Until the Department of Banking was set up, these requests came to the RBI, which used to informally consult the Finance Secretary on the advisability or otherwise of granting such permission. Much the same procedure applied when foreign banks wished to open branches in India. In 1975, BCCI, a bank with its main office in the United Arab Emirates (UAE) applied to the RBI for permission to open a branch in Bombay or Delhi. The RBI had not agreed on the ground that not all that bank's operations were legal or above board. However, for reasons of better political relations with the UAE, where a large number of Indians lived and worked, the Ministry of External Affairs was interested and wrote accordingly to the Finance Ministry. This provided an opportunity for the Department of Banking to cut into the powers of the RBI and get the Finance Minister to agree to a change of procedure. The secretary to that department wrote to the RBI governor that the Finance Minister had agreed that from now on, all requests from Indian banks for foreign branches or from foreign banks for Indian branches should go directly to the Finance Ministry, and that these would be considered by a committee in that department, consisting of its representative, together with the RBI and a representative of the External Affairs Ministry. Governor Puri did not raise any objection to this change of procedure, even though the Banking Regulation Act of 1969 had made the RBI the deciding authority. This was yet another encroachment on the RBI's powers, essentially for exercise of political authority.

IV

The intrusion of politics into banking affairs became even wider after the declaration of the Emergency. It soon became clear in the RBI that with the appointment of Puri as governor and Luther as his adviser, financial institutions had become an extension of the PMO – or even worse, of her close advisers. In 1976, the IDBI was de-linked from the RBI and its ownership transferred to the government. A new chairman loyal to the powers in New Delhi was appointed. Promotion of new enterprises with assistance from the IDBI and other banks became the monopoly of those loyal to the Prime Minister and her son. Mainly because of his disapproval of Sanjay Gandhi's doings, Haksar lost his position as the head of the PMO, and with it, deputy governor Hazari's hold on banking institutions diminished.

By the end of 1975, I was appointed a deputy governor. Puri's appointment as governor in August 1975 was not a development with which those in the Bank were happy. He had all along been in the life insurance business and hardly understood central banking. When one of the deputy governors retired in late 1975, someone else had to be appointed in his position. When I, along with P D Nangia (another ED in the Bank), was appointed, it was widely believed that it was Nangia and not me whom Puri had recommended. I was apparently the choice of Finance Minister C. Subramaniam. I had no way of knowing if that was what had happened; but if Puri was not happy about my appointment, he did not show it. Governor Puri quickly transferred the DBOD and credit planning from Hazari to me. However, by then the ARDC's responsibilities had expanded substantially and Hazari as head of that organisation went ahead to widen its scope and influence.

Governor Puri also decided to make Luther ED for the DBOD. Luther's contacts with Sanjay Gandhi and his associates were close, and instructions from this group usually reached Puri via him. However, when Luther sought to take some banking decisions on his own, I told him firmly that they had to be approved by me before issue. I also informed Puri accordingly and told him that when necessary I would consult him before issuing orders to the DBOD. For a while, relations between us were cool, but Puri quickly realised that the principal officers of the DBOD resented undue interference from Delhi in what they honestly believed to be the nation's central bank's domain.

At this juncture, the Central Bank of India, one of the important commercial banks (which had been nationalised in 1969), sought RBI approval for an additional loan of Rs 25 to Rs 30 lakh to the Maruti automobile company. This would have taken that bank's accommodation to the company well beyond Rs 1 crore, which was then the maximum that any bank could lend to a client without RBI approval. Knowing that Maruti had been set up by Sanjay Gandhi, the Chairman of the Central Bank of India was keen on securing RBI approval under the CAS. But this required a change in the RBI's policy of limiting individual loans for working capital purposes. Neither the DBOD nor the economic department was in favour of relaxing this limit as the creation of reserve money through budget deficits was already large and further credit creation would worsen the inflationary situation. Additional lending by commercial banks would inevitably lead to them borrowing from the RBI and neither department considered it necessary to relax the CAS limit. I wrote to the Central Bank of India accordingly, rejecting its application for the additional loan. The reaction from Delhi was immediate. Puri was told by the PMO that the loan must be sanctioned, by raising the CAS limit, which he promptly did without informing me or the DBOD. As governor, he had the authority to change any RBI policy, with of course the sanction of the central committee of the RBI board, which met every week. But he was in a hurry to conform to the requirements of Delhi. The departments under me were not informed about this change, nor were I and the central committee. I was naturally upset and told him that I no longer wanted to be in charge of the DBOD or the CPC. Puri was quick to assure me that it would not happen again and he would discuss things with me on all matters concerning credit policy. I waited for some weeks and when there was no other request for authorisation in excess of Rs 2 crore, I felt relieved. Apparently many others who had not approached the RBI for credit authorisation had secured advances in excess of Rs 1 crore. This may have been one reason for the rapid growth of bank credit after 1976.

There were soon other indications from Delhi that the Maruti affair was resented by the Prime Minister and her close advisers. Having got Puri to raise the CAS limit to Rs 2 crore, Sanjay Gandhi and his friends started borrowing freely from virtually every bank in Delhi, Haryana and Punjab. Loans, cash credits and overdrafts from commercial banks went up from Rs 7,055 crore in March 1975 to Rs 10,589 crore by December 1976 – an increase of nearly 50 per cent. That this was bound to happen was expected. The RBI's economic department was apprehensive of the later consequences of such a bank-supported increase in demand. However, the barrage of controls imposed on the community prevented undue stocking. During the Emergency, the wholesale price index, which had gone up to nearly 176 (base 1970-71=100) in April 1975, stayed around that level until March 1977. But after Indira Gandhi's defeat in the 1977 election and the advent of Morarji Desai's Janata government, the price index moved up by March 1980 to over 257,[2] partly due to the lifting of several controls and partly due to a poor harvest. During the Emergency, however, controls had been enforced strictly enough to hold prices, incomes and spending in check.

Within months of assuming office, Morarji Desai's government moved both Puri and Luther out of the RBI. Finance Minister H M Patel appointed I G Patel as the new governor, but he was unable to take charge until late that year and M Narasimham was sent from Delhi to hold temporary charge.[3] Reverting to the Emergency, pin-pricks in various ways continued throughout. Hazari's and my telephones were tapped and we had to issue instructions that no official matter should be discussed or communicated over the phone. Bank chairmen and senior officers of commercial banks, and our own staff were told to desist from resorting to phone calls. When Manmohan Singh as economic secretary in the Finance Ministry wanted some details from me, I asked him to send a telex or letter saying so. We also told the Banking Department that neither of us or our departments would accept telephonic requests or instructions. Later, when the new government instituted an enquiry in 1978 into RBI-government exchanges during Indira Gandhi's regime, these precautions came in handy. Two issues in particular caused considerable embarrassment to the Bank's exchange control and banking departments. One was the release of foreign exchange of $5 million to an official of the government's intelligence wing by Luther, apparently on telephonic instructions from Delhi, which was traced to the PMO. It was not clear if he had checked this with the governor or his deputy in charge of the exchange control department. Likewise, the substitution of Rs 2 crore for Rs 1 crore as the CAS limit in the DBOD's files was traced to Puri. The Janata government inquiry was fairly detailed, covering all departments. Commercial bank loans and foreign exchange allocations to those who were known to be close to Indira Gandhi or her son were specially scrutinised. Some of the information provided by this inquiry was later used in the unsuccessful arraignment in late 1977 of Indira Gandhi on charges of corruption and misuse of authority. That the trial fizzled out was another matter; but because of the precautions we had taken, neither of us was implicated in any way.

Even so, it took quite a while for Finance Minister H M Patel to accept my credentials. When Puri was removed and a temporary vacancy had to be filled, neither Hazari nor I was considered. Similarly, later on the position of executive director of the IMF was not offered to me and somebody else was chosen. These denials of important positions hurt me intensely and I was much tempted to resign from the RBI. But I could not do so as a variety of domestic problems had to be resolved and I was obliged to bide my time. But my heart was no longer in the job I was doing. The Finance Minister's prejudice against me persisted for many months until he came to know me (and about me from I G Patel). I discovered later that like many others, he believed that I had advised Asoka Mehta to accept devaluation.

V

For much of the Emergency, Subramaniam was Finance Minister. It was during his tenure that I was appointed a deputy governor despite Governor Puri's lack of support for me. The Finance Minister had got to know me when I was in the PC in the 1960s when he was a Cabinet member, first as Minister for Steel and then as Minister for Food and Agriculture. In the latter capacity, he was also a member of the PC and a confidant of Prime Minister Indira Gandhi. It was this earlier acquaintance with him which he remembered well enough to ask me to meet him in September 1975 in Delhi. I was an ED of the RBI then and I went to Delhi not knowing exactly why he wanted to see me. He had with him

R K Seshadri, who was the RBI's deputy governor concerned with the exchange control department, Manmohan Singh, the economic affairs secretary, and Vijay Joshi, an Oxford don who had been appointed adviser in the Finance Ministry. I found that the issue at that meeting was whether the rupee should continue to be linked to the pound sterling or go its own way on some other basis.

I had not expected to be involved in this matter and waited for the minister's opening remarks. Sometime before this meeting, V B Kadam, director of the economic department's balance of payments division, had told me that the rupee-sterling cross rate had come under pressure and the RBI had been obliged to intervene in the market to keep this under control. The pound sterling had depreciated significantly against the US dollar, as well as some other currencies. With its link to sterling, the rupee had also depreciated and the Finance Minister felt that some radical change in our exchange rate policy was needed. After some general discussion of the possibilities, the minister told Seshadri and me that a very limited group should examine the alternatives and come up with some definite advice on what would be best in the country's interest. He asked Seshadri to have this done in the RBI. He also asked Joshi to participate in further discussions on the ministry's behalf. These deliberations led to a change in India's exchange rate policy, from a link to some freely convertible hard currencies to one based on the values of a basket of currencies. The currencies chosen were naturally those of the country's major trading partners – the pound sterling, US dollar, Germany's deutschemark, the Swiss franc and the Japanese yen. These were among the currencies which the IMF had also chosen to work out the value of its SDR. The new policy became effective in September 1975. Though the contents of the basket were broadly known, the weight attached to each was a closely guarded secret. As the government's agent for managing the country's foreign exchange, the RBI had the responsibility of guarding this secret and adjusting the weights as and when necessary. The Indian rupee was technically on float; but the basket was in reality managed to provide some flexibility to the RBI. The government agreed that the basket value be maintained within a band of 2.25 per cent about the middle rate of Rs 18.31 per pound, which continued to be the intervention currency – that is, the currency which was used by the RBI for purchases and sales in the foreign exchange market. Because of frequent revisions in the rupee-pound rate, it was agreed with the government that the basket management be within a range of 5 per cent of the middle rate rather than 2.25 per cent as earlier stipulated. Until his retirement in July 1976, Seshadri had the main responsibility for all this as well as for management of the RBI's foreign assets. When he left office, the management of foreign assets became a part of my concerns. This involved daily decisions on how and where these assets should be invested, or whether any market intervention to maintain the basket value was needed. The section dealing with these matters was looked after by R Janakiraman, one of the Bank's ablest officers. He generally came over early in the morning to check how well or badly the exchange rates were doing in the eastern markets of Tokyo, Hong Kong and Singapore. He would then check with me if any adjustment in the basket value of the rupee was necessary, record my views and inform the RBI's other offices if any change in the rupee rate was indicated by the demand-supply equations of currencies in the basket. Later in the day, after the London financial market opened and the trends in asset values and interest rates were known, he would seek my concurrence on new investments or switches. Janakiraman soon moved up in the Bank's hierarchy, and during the rest of my term, A P Iyer was in charge of these operations. He kept to the same routine as his predecessor and took good care of the Bank's responsibilities. This reduced my daily involvement in this business and I could give full attention to other responsibilities in the RBI.

There were, however, two other operations connected with foreign trade and payments which straddled the economic and DBOD departments, both of which were under my charge. The years after 1974-75 witnessed a dramatic change in India's balance of payments, resulting in an accumulation of foreign exchange assets. This was mainly due to a substantial increase in net invisibles, together with increased foreign receipts from exports. This was contemporaneous with the shift to the basket rate of exchange, but not necessarily due to it. However, these adjustments had the effect of changing the business community's interest, as also that of the government, from import financing to export credits. At the government's request, a standing committee on export finance was set up under my chairmanship to deal with the extent of commercial bank financing of exports as also the terms on which they were provided. Banks were mostly engaged in providing "packing credit" to exporters, besides their normal borrowing for working capital purposes. By then, the government had set up the Export Credit Guarantee Corporation and the IDBI as entities separate from the RBI. Apart from the central Finance and Commerce ministries, the foreign exchange dealers' association was represented on this committee. From the RBI, both the exchange control department and the economic department sat along with me. By and large this committee focused on simplification of procedures as well as on cheapening of export finance provided by commercial banks. The committee met fairly frequently and its deliberations probably helped promote exports. It also enabled the government to provide some tax concessions besides direct subsidies, which had to be done without inviting adverse comments from the IMF or other governments.

While the government sought to enlarge export credits through the RBI, it followed a different course in certain other respects, bypassing the Bank altogether. This was a matter on which I was very sensitive. I tried to get Governor Puri to take a firm stand as it not only caused needless confusion in instructions to public-sector banks but adversely affected the Bank's policies of credit planning and monetary adjustments. It was also injurious to the RBI's standing in the financial world. Two direct instructions to public-sector banks from the Banking Department riled me in particular and I tried hard to get Puri to join issue with the Finance Minister on this tendency of its officials to bypass the Bank. The first was in connection with the 20-point programme. This was a favourite of Prime Minister Indira Gandhi and she wanted these measures to be taken up by the agencies concerned fully and quickly. Some of these related to extension of credit to bonded labour, small farmers, village industries like handlooms and so forth. Laudable as these objectives were, the RBI was upset by the Banking Department issuing orders directly to the SBI and other public-sector banks rather than through it, as was the usual practice. Likewise, the Banking Department wrote to public-sector banks raising their lending to priority sectors from around the prevailing level of 25 per cent of total credit to 33⅓ per cent within a year. Considering that priority sectors included both small farmers and small businesses or industries in rural areas, the RBI was not opposed to such a move; a committee under my chairmanship actually suggested some time later an overall target of 40 per cent of total credit. What was objectionable was the Banking Department issuing orders to the SBI and other public-sector banks ignoring the RBI and its credit policy and planning objectives. Despite my strong urging, Governor Puri failed to raise this issue with the government. He also prevented me from writing on this matter to the officials concerned or raising it during our discussions with the Finance Minister. It was not until after the 1977 elections that the relations between the RBI and the Banking Department changed and the Bank's primacy in matters of credit policy was accepted by the Finance Minister.

The subterranean feud between the RBI and the Banking Department had existed since the latter's inception in 1968, in a somewhat mild way. But it came into the open and challenging after the nationalisation of the major public-sector banks in 1969 and the status of the Banking Department was raised by appointing A Bakshi as a full secretary in that department. Disagreements between Governor Jagannathan and Hazari in the RBI and Bakshi were frequent. This got worse under N C Sen Gupta, in whose term the government started asserting its rights as owner of public-sector banks, despite the Banking Regulation Act of 1969 making it abundantly clear that all powers of direction and inspection of banks were vested with the Reserve Bank. As Prime Minister Indira Gandhi became more authoritarian after the 1971 elections, the Banking Department also became more strident. By the time I became deputy governor, Narasimham had taken over as that department's secretary and his minions became more interfering. Narasimham's attitude towards me had always been one of subdued hostility and this became more evident as officers under him went about throwing their weight on the managements of public sector banks. Governor Puri, who was totally ignorant of banking affairs and policy, made it easier for the Banking Department by not asserting the statutory powers enjoyed by the RBI. This went on until Puri was relieved of his office by the new Finance Minister in 1977. Because of the hiatus between Puri's departure and assumption by I G Patel of the governorship, Narasimham came in for a few months as governor. Before this, there had been considerable speculation in Bombay's banking circles that either Hazari or I would be put in charge of the RBI.

But it was not to be. Whether this was due to Hazari's earlier association with Indira Gandhi or closeness to Haksar, or my unearned reputation for favouring devaluation, or even Narasimham's wangling for the job, one does not know. In the few months of his governorship, Narasimham's health was poor and he was often hospitalised. Hazari had also been advised to avoid over-exertion because of a cardiac problem. The result was that despite my own failing health, nearly all policy decisions had to be taken by me. This could be managed only because of the efficiency and devotion of most chief officers of the several departments – and my instructions to them to refer things to me only when some discussion with the Finance Ministry was necessary. Since Morarji Desai's new government which took office in 1977 was a patched-up coalition, Delhi was fully occupied with sorting out its own problems and it was not until later that the RBI drew its attention. But before the end of 1977, I G Patel took over as governor, and my responsibilities lessened. He and Finance Minister H M Patel had worked together in the 1950s when the latter was the Finance Secretary. It was not until early 1978 that I had a chance to go to Delhi with I G Patel for a discussion with the Finance Minister. This concerned certain issues connected with the opening of Indian branches of foreign banks as well as adjustments in the rates of interest admissible on Indian deposits by NRIs. Both these were matters on which the DBOD as well as the CPC were concerned. That meeting cleared any doubts the Finance Minister might have had about my integrity and competence; from then on, he often invited me to dinner at his house, where I had the chance of often meeting Varghese Kurien of the "White Revolution" fame.

NOTES

1 Apart from the State Bank of India which had been taken over by the RBI in 1956.

2 *Handbook of Statistics on Indian Economy*, RBI (1999), p 47.

3 This was not to either Hazari's or my liking, but the Finance Ministry had got used to preferring its secretaries to senior deputy governors for even temporary appointments. Both Hazari and I were unhappy because within the RBI cadre, Narasimham was junior to both of us. He had worked under Hazari and had opted to move over to Delhi when I took charge.

8

Retirement and After

I

APART from vicissitudes in my personal affairs, there was nothing particularly significant in terms of institutional change or public policy with which I was associated in the final years of my tenure in the RBI. By late 1977, when I G Patel took over as governor, my health had deteriorated and my visits to Delhi or other offices of the RBI became infrequent. This was also due partly to the increasing emphasis on fiscal policy to which the Government of India had recourse. The process which had started with the nationalisation of commercial banks in 1969 by Indira Gandhi had led to a downgrading of most public institutions, including the IAS and other services. The RBI was no exception, and this trend had continued under the Janata government of 1977-79. Even matters on which the RBI technically had a measure of statutory authority were not left unaffected. Deputy Prime Minister Charan Singh, who was in charge of the finance portfolio, announced reductions of commercial bank lending rates in his 1979 budget speech. His predecessors had refrained from doing so even if there was the need for it, leaving things to the discretion of the RBI. This incursion was in addition to the encroachment on credit policy as a result of the 20-point programme of the Emergency period. Charan Singh's foray into interest rate policy had gone well beyond Indira Gandhi's interference with commercial banks' credit policy.

That Governor Patel did not formally protest against this encroachment surprised me – indeed all my colleagues in the Bank. A little before this, he had modified the extent to which the central government could borrow from the market, much to my chagrin. When the budget was being discussed in early 1979, I had got the Finance Secretary to agree that government borrowing during 1979-80 would not exceed Rs 200 crore. This was on the ground that any further increase would adversely affect the cost of borrowing by state governments as well as by public or private enterprises. On my return to Bombay, I had told I G Patel of this agreement with the Finance Secretary, as well as my reasons for it. However, when he went later for a final discussion of the budget details, he agreed to raise this amount to Rs 400 crore. He had, of course, the authority to overrule me. But I did not like his doing so, without so much as a word to me. Having been friends with him for long, I made no secret of my displeasure – nor did he misconstrue this.

The onslaughts on what legitimately constituted the RBI's domain must have disturbed him as well. But the Janata government did not last long enough to damage the Bank's position further. Morarji Desai and Charan Singh were engaged in a power struggle, which occupied all their attention. Several of the constituents of that government moved away, as a general election became a distinct possibility. With the government on its last legs, policy decisions remained unattended, and I G Patel was left undisturbed. Even the Banking Department refrained from interfering with credit policy, though it continued to deal with administrative matters of public-sector banks. It was also a period in which the RBI could hardly move ahead in any significant way.

It was not long before Indira Gandhi came back to power and R Venkataraman took charge as Finance Minister. Indira Gandhi soon resumed her old ways of concentrating all authority in the Prime Minister, though she did not disturb I G Patel's governorship. Apart from pushing her 20-point programme on public-sector banks, and appointing her cronies to the boards of these banks, she did not meddle in matters of credit or banking policy. This may have been due to her familiarity with I G Patel (who had served her in the Finance Ministry earlier); or because of the tragic death of her son Sanjay Gandhi in an air accident and the relative quiescence of her cronies.

Finance Minister Venkataraman was not aggressive like his predecessors, and tended to be formal in his relations with I G Patel and the RBI. He came over to Bombay for a day, during which he met the principal officers of the Bank, as well as of the IDBI and the chief executives of both public and private banks. His colourless tenure might not have continued for long had Indira Gandhi not been deeply involved in the Punjab problem. Taking advantage of the initial support extended to him by Indira Gandhi, Jarnail Singh Bhindranwale had built himself up as a militant leader of Sikhs, and started agitating for a separate Sikh nation named Khalistan. His followers resorted to a series of terrorist attacks on the police and on prominent Hindus, especially editors of some of the newspapers in Amritsar. These led to what has since become notorious as Operation Blue Star, the storming of the Golden Temple and the Akal Takht complex by the army, a measure which virtually turned the entire Sikh community against Indira Gandhi. This culminated in her assassination in October 1984. Infuriated by this, Congressmen closely associated with her decimated the Sikhs in Delhi and other Hindu strongholds. It was a madness which resembled the massacre of Sikhs at Jallianwala Bagh during British rule (and the later massacre of Muslims in Gujarat in 2002). Following Indira Gandhi's killing, the President quickly nominated her son Rajiv Gandhi to the prime ministership, probably in the hope that he would take steps to stop the carnage, but nothing of the sort happened to his everlasting discredit.

All this was, however, after my retirement from the RBI, which was due at the end of December 1980. Early that month, I had a cardiac disability, which kept me in bed for some weeks and I could not send in my papers in time. Perhaps to enable me to rest in Bombay, I G Patel asked me to continue until my successor was named. But I was not prepared to do so and told him that I would stay only until 31 March 1981. I requested him to inform the Government of India accordingly, which he did.

II

Leaving all that aside, the 1970s was in many ways a period of singular achievements, as well as of singular failures, for the Bank. Until 1975, there was a remarkable expansion of banking in India, especially of the SBI, and other public-sector banks. The RBI was more or less left undisturbed by the government, thanks largely to Hazari's endeavours. Neither the governor nor the PMO interfered with his policy of obliging public-sector banks to open three branches in rural or semi-urban locations before seeking a licence for an office in a city or metropolitan area. Hazari toured the states to work out with the governments concerned the specific locations where banks could open rural branches. He was fully supported by officers of the DBOD and other departments under him, including the ARDC. This policy of public-sector banks having to pay special attention to the needs of India's rural sector continued throughout the 1970s. It was only later that the pressure on banks to heed the needs of agriculture and other rural activities was eased.

However, these achievements were overshadowed by two major developments during that period. First, several of the institutions established and nurtured by the RBI in the 1960s and 1970s were delinked and set up as independent entities controlled directly by the government. This included the IDBI and the UTI, both of which had been set up under the aegis of RBI in 1964. These institutions – to the development of which the RBI had provided both financial and personnel support – were taken over by the Ministry of Finance, though a substantial part of the RBI's profits continued to be transferred to the Long-Term Industries Fund, from which the IDBI could borrow. It became more cumbersome for the RBI to work out a tenable relationship between short- and long-term interest rates or a uniform leveraging factor. The UTI ceased to be the concern of the RBI and became answerable to the IDBI on matters of policy. Its chairman was appointed by the government (as in the case of the IDBI). It also named one of its principal officers as the UTI's executive trustee – a function which I used to carry out as an executive director of the Bank.

The separation of the IDBI and the UTI from the RBI imposed some limitations on the Bank's coordination function. However, this was of less concern than the second debilitating factor, the progressive narrowing of the Bank's domain, and a decline of its independence in deciding monetary and credit policies. The slow rot had really started in the mid-1950s with the conversion of the Imperial Bank of India to the SBI. However, this institution was owned by the RBI, though its chief executive was a government appointee. More importantly, things came to a head with the resignation of Governor B Rama Rau. I was away in the US when this happened and cannot fully vouch for what happened. What I gathered from colleagues in the Bank later was that it was a case of conflict between the RBI's monetary policy and the government's legitimate desire to mobilise resources for the Second Five-Year Plan. The governor resigned because he felt that the

RBI's autonomy on monetary policy had been seriously compromised by this levy.[1] This conflict between the objective of anti-inflationary monetary policy and garnering adequate financial resources for economic development remains a continuing problem for the RBI.

The next foray by New Delhi into banking affairs was in terms of "social banking" and priority sectors. A little before nationalisation of the major commercial banks in 1969, the general feeling was that banking facilities were unevenly distributed and that large sections of the rural community were not adequately served by organised financial institutions. Cooperative institutions in virtually all states had ceased to be entitled to the refinance facilities which the RBI was required to provide. Save for the extension of branch facilities by the SBI and its associate banks, most commercial banks operated in mainly urban areas and concentrated on short-term finance needed by industrial and commercial borrowers. Large sections of farmers and small enterprises in rural areas had no alternative to borrowing at usurious rates of interest from private moneylenders. Also, most commercial bank branches were concentrated in the northern, western and southern states leaving large parts of the central and eastern states unserved. It was largely to remedy this uneven distribution of bank branches that the government resorted to social banking, paying special attention to the credit requirements of rural areas, especially in the principally agricultural areas of Uttar Pradesh, Madhya Pradesh, Rajasthan, Bihar, Orissa, West Bengal and the North-Eastern states. However, it was not until after bank nationalisation that banking policy (of both the government and the RBI) changed materially towards rapid expansion of facilities in rural areas.

As mentioned earlier, there was no conflict between the RBI and the government in the initial part of the 1970s. By and large, the newly established Department of Banking in the Finance Ministry went along with the branch banking policy of the RBI. It was only with the Emergency that the relations between the two soured. Chief executives of banks, whose tenure in office depended on decisions by the Banking Department, started dealing directly with New Delhi on issues other than purely administrative ones. I have referred earlier to the 20-point programme which was being pushed by government. Since this dealt mainly with disadvantaged sections of the community – like marginal farmers, bonded labour and so forth – the RBI saw no reason to object.

III

However, before my departure from the Bank, a series of disagreements between the RBI and the government arose, largely due to moves by the Department of Banking. A major issue, mentioned earlier, had to do with the opening of branches of Indian banks in foreign countries and of branches of foreign banks in India. It led to public-sector banks formally sending their requests to the Finance Ministry after 1975 instead of writing to the RBI. Governor Puri acquiesced in the altered procedure without demur. By then, the DBOD had prepared, at my instance, a perspective plan on possible locations for foreign branches of Indian banks, which had broadly been approved by the Bank's central committee. When the Finance Ministry convened the next meeting in 1977, the Janata government had assumed office in Delhi and Manmohan Singh was in charge of economic affairs and Shroff had become additional secretary in the Banking Department. With the DBOD's perspective plan in hand, I attended the inter-departmental committee meeting in New Delhi on behalf of the Bank. There was much less disagreement in that meeting and most of the foreign locations in which banks wished to open branches were approved. However, this turned out to be transient. In subsequent meetings of this committee, which a relatively junior officer of the DBOD attended, the Finance or External Affairs ministries had their way.

Leaving this aside, the basic reason for gradual downgrading of the Bank as well as of monetary policy was the continuing pressure for resource mobilisation for development plans adopted by the government. This started with the Second Five-Year Plan, during which the government sought to restructure the economy through heavy public investments in basic and capital goods industries. The accumulated sterling balances had been used up, and agreement with the US for use of PL 480 funds for local expenditure had not yet been reached. For collecting additional resources, the Finance Minister levied, in 1956, a stamp duty on bills of exchange, as mentioned earlier. A similar situation of inadequate foreign exchange and domestic resources led to the substitution of annual plans for five-year plans between 1966 and 1969, devaluation and other consequences. With the resumption of five-year plans in 1969-70, fiscal pressure on resource mobilisation became intense. These were also years of increased defence outlays because of war with Pakistan and the emergence of Bangladesh. All told, in the 1970s, the government began viewing commercial bank deposits as a national resource which, one way or another, could be tapped for national development. The first attempt for this purpose was the Differential Rate of Interest scheme (DRI scheme) to benefit the poorer segments of society, particularly poor farmers, SCs and STs, and so forth. By then the major commercial banks had been nationalised and the Finance Ministry took this up as a socially desirable objective, especially suited to the needs of the vulnerable in rural communities. However, neither the RBI nor the public-sector banks were prepared to set apart more than a small portion of their advances for this purpose. Banks were already committed to providing advances at concessional rates to the "priority sectors", and the DRI scheme became part and parcel of that allocation.

More significant than this limited direction of bank advances was the continuing increase in the SLR. As the central government's plans became bigger, the SLR also went up, reaching 35 per cent of total deposits of banks by the late 1970s. As part of its anti-inflationary policy, the RBI also raised the Cash Reserve Ratio (CRR) to 6 per cent of total deposit liabilities. Altogether, more than 40 per cent of banks' deposit resources had to be made over either to the RBI or invested in government and trustee securities. This was roughly the position when I left the RBI in March 1981.

There was another development in the 1970s that was noteworthy. When the green revolution led to a massive increase in wheat and rice output in the late 1960s, the FCI was established to buy large quantities of the foodgrains at minimum support prices announced by the government from year to year. Since the stocks were to be distributed through the PDS or fair price shops at specified prices, provision of "food credit" to the FCI became part and parcel of banking advances. Virtually all public-sector banks, including the SBI group, were required to participate in a consortium to provide food credit. Likewise, when crude oil prices suddenly flared up in 1973, the RBI presided over a consortium of banks which was required to meet the needs of the nationalised oil refineries. Yet another instance of public needs having to be satisfied was additional imports of fertilisers, the demand for which had increased manifold as the green revolution spread to rice and cotton and so forth. The Bank's responsibilities to direct commercial bank advances to these specific requirements, as well as to public enterprises like Bharat Heavy Electricals Ltd (BHEL), had become quite extensive. But it is only fair to say that, save for food credit, there was no government pressure for concessional finance.

Meanwhile, under an act passed during the Emergency, Regional Rural Banks (RRBs) had been set up to cater specifically for the needs of rural areas, especially those of small and marginal farmers. The initiative for this had come from the Department of Banking, largely through additional secretary Narasimham. The RRBs were to be sponsored by one of the public-sector banks and their operations confined to one (or more) districts, with the freedom to open branches wherever they deemed fit. The initial capital, as well as the managerial personnel, was to be provided by the sponsor bank. Besides mobilising rural deposits, these banks were required to lend at suitable rates to local users of finance for their productive or marketing operations. The RBI disfavoured the idea of cooperative institutions also sponsoring RRBs. On whether the rural branches of the sponsor banks, or of other banks operating in the area, should be made over to the local RRBs, the view within the RBI, as well as among specialists concerned, was that the choice should be left to the sponsor banks; no general policy decision was taken.

In essence, the RRBs were intended to encourage both deposit mobilisation and additional loans to agriculture and other rural activities. For this purpose, somewhat higher rates were to be paid on local deposits, and the deposits so mobilised were to be loaned mostly to local businesses. Since the alternative source of loans was often the moneylender or local trader, who usually charged very high rates of interest, it was believed that RRBs could lend at somewhat higher rates than what commercial bank branches charged, but not higher than those charged by cooperative institutions operating in their areas. The RBI also stipulated somewhat lower rates of SLR and CRR for the RRBs – lower than those specified for commercial banks in general. It had been suggested that the pay scales of the staff should be on par with those of the state government in the area the bank was in. However, all this changed subsequently, as even before I left, the RRBs had begun to feel that they were as much a part of the organised financial system as commercial banks and saw no reason for any discrimination.

IV

At the same time as my appointment as deputy governor in December 1975, I was informed by Bhabhatosh Datta, a distinguished professor from Calcutta, that I was to succeed him as president of the Indian Economic Association (IEA) for the following year, that is, 1976. At that time, P R Brahmananda, professor and head of the economics department in Bombay University, managed the routine affairs of the IEA and also edited its journal. This helped me avoid getting involved in the association's routine activities such as convening periodic meetings of the managing committee and the like. All I was required to do was preside over the association's annual meeting in December 1976, elect the following year's office-bearers, and deliver the annual address. Much to my satisfaction, the next year's session was to be held in Mysore by the University of Mysore, my alma mater. Despite 1976 having been a difficult year for me for several reasons, I decided to delve deep into inflation and the role of monetary policy in my presidential address.

These were recurrent topics wherever I served and I had thought about them for several years. Because of my years in the PC and the RBI, I had tried to look at more than one aspect of the problem – as a monetary phenomenon and also as a resource mobilisation issue. I had often asked myself the question: are price increases necessarily bad? Obviously consumers felt that every price increase meant a reduction in the real value of their money incomes, and so resented them. But the consumers often wore a different cap professionally, that is, as producers, traders, financiers, commission agents and so on, and in that capacity often benefited from price rises. Viewed differently, while consumers desired the policymakers to ensure either stable (or very slow rising) prices, the class of producers desired steadily rising prices to facilitate additional production and/or investment. In other words, not all sections of the community, nor all categories of income-earners, viewed price changes the same way. This was an aspect of which I had become acutely conscious; the more I thought about it, the more aware I had become of the important effect that institutions (using the term in its widest connotation) had on both the phenomenon of price changes and on those deciding on social, political or economic policies. No society is, or can be, homogeneous. Inevitably, group interests develop for economic or historical reasons, and those who decide on policy (especially in a democratic or free-market set-up) have to seek ways and means of avoiding antagonising any of these groups. Recognising all these as part of my own experience, I wrote out "Thoughts on Inflation and Distribution" as the presidential address to the IEA (see Appendix I).

That was the first of the speeches I had to deliver in the 1970s. Over the next five years, especially after the lifting of the Emergency in 1977, there were occasions for me to deliver addresses on topics of essentially economic import. In all these, I kept returning to the divergence between macro-concepts and micro-realities. It is the latter of which political operators or social scientists were better aware than the economic theorist. As questions such as poverty, unemployment, class distinctions, and professional diversities became clearer in my own reckoning, macro-economic categorisations of "income", "saving", "consumption", and "investment" became less useful than social diversities or sectional interests. More often than not, I found myself thinking in terms of specific categories or segments of society, which needed special attention than the generality of consumers or producers. Thus on one occasion, I talked about surpluses in the economy that were helpful, such as food or foreign exchange surpluses; or on other occasions of the future of India's banking industry; and the strengths and weaknesses of public enterprises, which had by then become an integral part of India's industrial structure. In each of these cases, it was again the institutional factors which seemed to account for the prevalent behaviour pattern of political leaders or principal administrators.

But it was mainly monetary policy in its various phases, and the question of RBI autonomy that kept recurring ever so often during the rest of the 1970s and the early 1980s. Towards the fag end of my term in the RBI, I was invited by the Maharaja Sayajirao University of Baroda to deliver a memorial lecture and I used that opportunity to put together my thoughts on "The Limits of Monetary Policy". The provocation for this was a conditional loan of 5 billion SDRs from the IMF under its Extended Fund Facility. In seeking this accommodation, the government had agreed to a series of conditions imposed by the IMF on both demand and supply management. While the RBI had to control the magnitudes of both "narrow" and "broad" monetary aggregates as part of demand management, supply management was something else. This was mainly the responsibility of the central and state governments but partly also that of the private sector. This sector naturally desired liberalisation of credit facilities by the RBI – and the Bank found it difficult to ride the two horses of demand and supply management simultaneously. The IMF had also stipulated that the total of budgetary deficits should be limited to some specified proportion of GDP together with a series of conditions on tax and monetary policies. However, having agreed to lend a massive amount of SDRs, the Fund had to accept substantial incurring of payments deficits – the obverse of which was the inflow of domestic currency to the RBI. Much of the import surplus was incurred to add to domestic supplies of articles of mass consumption. Altogether, the early 1980s were not an easy period either for the Government of India or for the RBI.

It was against this background that I cogitated on the relevance of limits to monetary policy. It was clear that the RBI's capacity to vary money supply was quite limited for various reasons, and even instruments at its disposal to adjust the quantity of the community's exchange media had an uncertain impact. The community's other characteristics – such as income distribution, consumer preferences and expectations, propensities to save or hoard liquidity, market imperfections, and so on – influenced the income velocity of money supply in ways which could not be pre-determined or even forecast reasonably well. Over and above all this, budgetary and balance of payments conditions caused major variations in money supply over the year. Apart from its ability to alter discount facilities, commercial banks' deposit or lending rates, SLR and CRR, the RBI's means of varying money stock could only have a limited effect on monetary circulation, on its transactions and income velocity. The RBI's ability to operate somewhat more effectively its open market operations was much less in the 1970s and early 1980s than it is currently. There has since been a major expansion of the government bond market; and together with the Fiscal Reforms and the Budgetary Management Act of 2002, the Bank's ability to indulge in open market operations to vary money supply effectively has improved somewhat. Even so, there is no way of forecasting whether and in what ways changes in money supply could materially affect prices or price expectations. It was on this theme that I dwelt at some length in my lecture at the Baroda university (see Appendix II).

It was some time after I left the RBI that its golden jubilee was celebrated (in 1985) and the then Governor Manmohan Singh commissioned E P W da Costa to write the 50-year story. Da Costa's little volume was so slight and disappointing that I was urged to write a scathing review of the book. What had been left out – perhaps for reasons other than that of presenting the historical truth objectively – was the stupendous decline in the Bank's ability to act with any degree of autonomy in matters concerning monetary and banking policy. I could not resist the desire to set out my feelings on that subject. In the nearly 30 years of my service in the Bank, I had witnessed the progressive dominance of the government over banking affairs, and save for a solitary protest in the mid-1950s, this loss of autonomy evoked no resistance from any of the governors, virtually all of whom were government appointees (see Appendix III). Rereading that review now, I realise, however, that the concept of the central bank's independence of action had never been a reality, for the simple reason that in every country the government has clearly to be the final authority on all matters. It could not have been otherwise, and the so-called autonomy of the central bank amounted to nothing more than a voluntary delegation of specific privileges to it. When things altered to make fiscal policy a determining factor, especially in a developing economy, it was inevitable for monetary policy to be relegated to a secondary, and supportive, role. What happened with the RBI was no more than a historical necessity.

V

Following my retirement in 1981, I shifted to Bangalore, where most members of my family lived. Some years earlier, I had managed to build a house for us in a newly developed extension of the city. This was possible largely because of the efforts of my friend Eknath Kamath, who was then the CMD of Canara Bank, one of the public-sector banks. After the hectic years in the PC and the RBI, I looked forward to my retirement. I hoped to enjoy the rest and to catch up with my reading, especially of Kannada literature, which had been transformed in the previous three decades. I also planned to recover from the cardiac damage I had suffered in the latter half of the 1970s. But as things turned out, this was not to be; somewhat reluctantly I agreed to participate in a few seminars on public policy organised by the local Institute for Social and Economic Change. But one thing led to another, and soon I was up to my ears in such functions. It was not until after the turn of the century, that I could enjoy relative leisure. The only commitment which lasted a few years after 2000 was membership of the Sameeksha Trust (of which later).

A little after I moved to Bangalore, Governor I G Patel asked me to head a committee to review the working of the National Institute of Bank Management (NIBM), Pune. The other members of the committee were O P Gupta, who was earlier head of the Punjab National Bank, and V S Vyas, a distinguished economist from the University in Jaipur. We were to submit our report in three or four months, during which time we visited Bombay and Pune and interviewed some bankers and academicians. We submitted our report to the RBI governor before the stipulated period. I did not follow up what action was taken on our report.

Early in 1982, I was invited for a few months by the EDI in Washington DC, of which I had been director from 1967 to 1972. The EDI's director at that time was an Indian. He wanted me to go over for some months and prepare reading material for the participants on the Indian experience of co-ordinating monetary and fiscal policies. He also hoped to invite all past directors of the EDI to come over and review what the institute was doing and what else could be done to add to its usefulness to developing countries. Since the invitation was an opportunity to renew old friendships and also visit our children in Nevada and Arizona, my wife and I decided to accept it. I do not realise then that it could lead to a succession of similar assignments over the next two decades.

Several assignments from international organisations followed – an invitation from the Asian Development Bank in Manila to prepare a report on "Domestic Resource Mobilisation through

Financial Development" in 1983; and a request from the UN Group of 77 in New York for drafting the scheme for a South Bank (to provide long-term development assistance to its members like the World Bank). This was followed by a meeting of experts to consider that draft in New York. A second request from the Asian Development Bank to prepare the country report on India on savings mobilisation through financial development was followed by short visits to Manila for discussions on similar reports. There was finally an invitation from the Organisation for Economic Coordination and Development (OECD) in Paris for planning a study programme on trade and development. These jaunts were periodic and usually lasted for no more than a few days or weeks. They were useful in keeping me abreast of world events; but they did not engage my main attention, which after 1983 was occupied mostly with being a member of the Karnataka government's economic and planning council.

In the election to the Karnataka State Assembly in 1983, the Janata Dal won a majority and Ramakrishna Hegde, a charismatic leader, was chosen to head the state government. He had been a close associate of the late JP, who had successfully agitated against Indira Gandhi in the early 1970s. Though the Indian Constitution clearly separated the powers of the central and state governments, Indira Gandhi had dominated the constituent states and encroached on their authority. Hegde resented this and decided to fight it. As a first step, he convened an all-India seminar on centre-state relations, essentially to strike at the centre's tendency to override the states. More than 100 social scientists, jurists, political analysts, media persons and social reformers were brought over to Bangalore for the discussion. At that juncture, a commission under Justice Sarkaria had been appointed by the Government of India on inter-governmental issues. Two members of that commission also attended the seminar as observers. Hegde had asked me to organise this seminar with the help of two young officers of his administration. Its conclusions were widely publicised, affecting both public opinion and subsequent developments. Organising these discussions in Bangalore were not easy, but Hegde's government provided every kind of assistance necessary and I found it a deeply satisfying effort.

Following this, Hegde went on to get the state assembly to pass the Panchayat Institutions Act in 1983, providing for decentralised governments at the district and *mandal* (a group of adjacent villages) levels. At the *mandal* level, the panchayat members were elected on the basis of adult franchise. This body was entrusted with the responsibility for planning and executing the development works needed, for which specific budgetary allocations were made in the state budget.

The economic and planning council of Karnataka played a not inconsiderable part in giving final touches to the Panchayat Raj Act of 1983 as well as the rules and regulations under the Act. The main architect and promoter of that legislation was Nazir Sab, who was the Rural Development Minister. He had to steer the Bill through the State Assembly without the support of some of his powerful colleagues, especially Minister for Public Works H D Deve Gowda. In the council meetings, which debated different aspects of the Bill, in particular the devolution of administrative authority to panchayats at the district or village levels, Deve Gowda refused to put the district authorities of his department under the chief secretaries of district panchayats. Some years later, he broke away from Hegde and headed a separate segment of the Janata Party. The council was however not distracted by Deve Gowda and proceeded to set out in some detail the full scheme of devolution to the new institutions.

Despite its very successful inauguration in 1987 through a statewide election, Karnataka's panchayat raj institutions (PRIs) have had a chequered history. When P S Appu, L C Jain and I went round the state in 1989 to report on how the PRIs were working, we found it was a mixed picture – some were performing excellently while many others had found it difficult to accept the dual system operating in the districts. While the panchayat institutions looked after development tasks in the districts, the purely revenue and administrative responsibilities continued to be looked after by the deputy commissioners (who was also the district magistrates) and their subordinates at the taluk and village levels. The three of us commented on the problem created by this duality and suggested a series of measures to set this right by a progressive transfer of administrative responsibilities to the panchayats, together with a transfer of budgetary resources. However, before our recommendations could be adopted, Karnataka was put under governor's rule, followed by an election in which the Congress Party returned to power, and started a systematic reversal of the devolutionary process. PRIs have ceased to be what the council had hoped they would ultimately be, bringing government closer to the people and creating a truly democratic polity. Though an amendment of the Constitution provided for a third tier of government at the sub-state level in the early 1990s, really effective institutions have not come into being. But that is a different story which does not belong here.

Apart from becoming somewhat involved in the state government's affairs, I also ventured into the private corporate sector during the 1980s and 1990s. The initial step in this direction was when I was made chairman of Grindlays Bank's advisory committee. I was also inducted, with permission from the RBI, onto the boards of directors of several corporate enterprises – some on behalf of the IDBI but most on the request of the chief executives of those companies. It was a mixed bag of companies of which I found myself a director, from finance to power stations to pharmaceuticals to cables to marketing. In all of these, my experience was not such as to add to my respect for the corporate sector. The CMDs of these enterprises, and their next-in-command, rarely shared the details of their business with the directors. Even when the board met every month, meetings barely lasted more than an hour, during which only a few items on the agenda were discussed. Notes on agenda items were brief and not very informative about sales proceeds, staff expenses and other cost details. Very little of substance was reported and there was no way in which they could be scrutinised in depth. On the whole, most meetings were mainly occasions for some general discussion, the payment of sitting fees or the distribution of some small gifts.

The CMDs usually did not have a majority interest in the company. Debt-equity ratios were usually high and there was rarely a systematic plan to bring this ratio down to a sustainable level. Save for the professional staff, the recruitment procedures were hazy and often those appointed to important positions in the company tended to be close relatives or confidants of the CMD or his senior staff. Most important, one discovered too late in the day that neither a company's accounts nor its cost-accounting was reflective of its true position. Obviously, many details were fudged and one was never sure how well or badly the enterprise was doing. With regard to transparency and open access to details, the private corporate sector was no better than the public sector, which was traditionally secretive. It was not a happy experience I had with business enterprises and I resigned from these directorships after some years. That did not mean, however, that I was rid of them altogether. Some continued to bother me for years afterwards.

The Grindlays Bank connection had led me to the international advisory board of the Australia and New Zealand Bank (ANZ Bank), which had bought the Indian business of Grindlays some years earlier. My colleagues on the ANZ board were senior businessmen or political figures from Europe, the USA or Australia and New Zealand where the ANZ Bank operated. These meetings were not very frequent and were held in a different country on each alternate occasion. The bank's headquarters being Melbourne in Australia, we used to meet there more frequently. During the five years I was on that board, we had meetings in London, New York, Frankfurt, Auckland and New Delhi. More than anything, these were occasions for discussion of banking trends in different countries as well as of trade and economic policies. Most of my colleagues on the board being from developed countries, their interest was in trade liberalisation and market freedoms. I was the only member from a developing country in which the state had assumed heavy development responsibilities. They often tried to persuade me of the benefits of the free-market system, globalisation and so forth. Much to their satisfaction, India's "reforms" also became a reality after 1991. Though I had by then no contact with the Government of India, I still believed in the dominant role to be played by the state in the country's development. My colleagues on the board thought they had played some part in converting the Indian government, a notion of which I did not try to disabuse them. My membership of this advisory group ended in 1993, after which I gradually gave up my involvement in state or local activities of an academic or political nature.

One relationship which I could not terminate by the mid-1990s was that with the *EPW*. As I mentioned at the outset, this connection with the well-known journal started in the mid-1940s, as soon as I went to Bombay to join the University School of Economics and Sociology. That was before the *EPW*'s predecessor, the *EW* was started by Sachin and his brother Hiten. When I joined the RBI in 1952, my links with the journal became stronger. My wife and I shared Sachin's apartment with him for some months and I wrote out pieces which he polished up before publication. It was not the best of times for the *EW*; it could hardly get any advertisements or engage adequately paid correspondents. But the journal quickly gained a reputation among economists and social scientists, many of whom contributed highly original articles, which drew international attention, to it. Some of India's eminent economists, current or prospective, encouraged Sachin, and in turn were encouraged by him, to keep going. He carried on until the mid-1960s when the *EW* literally ran out of funds and folded up.

However, Sachin was not to be daunted by this contretemps. Together with P B Gajendragadkar, a former chief justice of India, and H T Parekh, a prominent financier, he formed the Sameeksha Trust, which mobilised enough resources to start the successor to the *EW*, the *EPW*. The new journal carried on the job of creating social ferment and encouraging intellectual curiosity, as the *EW* had done before it. Sachin did not, however, live long enough to nurture the *EPW* through its infancy. He died in December 1966, just months after the *EPW* came into existence in August 1966.

By the time *EPW* started publication, Sachin and the *EW* had both become well known in the intellectual circles of India as well as English-speaking countries. The journal's editorials and notes on current affairs became distinguished for two reasons – they did not promote any special or partisan interest; and they and the special articles each issue contained, provided enough intellectual content to satisfy the researcher as also the social reformer. Sachin's eclectic approach created enormous goodwill for the journal among policymakers, social scientists and the vast majority of students in universities or special institutions.

Sachin's death meant that a new editor had to be found to run the *EPW* and the Sameeksha Trust entrusted the responsibility to R K Hazari, a professor in one of the local colleges who had done much research on Indian industries. When this change occurred, I was away and was not sure if the Sameeksha Trust had done the right thing. My doubts arose from what I knew of Hazari's concerns and political attitudes. I believed that he had a bias against large business houses. But before I returned to the RBI in 1972, he had moved over as deputy governor there. The new editor was Krishna Raj, whom I had known earlier as a student of the Delhi School of Economics, and more importantly as Sachin's technical assistant in the *EW*'s office.

In his dedication and objectivity, Krishna Raj was no less committed to the *EPW* than was Sachin to *EW*. He valued Sachin's original intentions of promoting social education as well as young and upcoming social scientists. He was of course more than slightly left-oriented; but as editor, he was scrupulous in keeping the columns of the *EPW* open to all schools of thought. No matter what the individual contribution's political philosophy or ethical or aesthetic values were, the *EPW* provided space for their expression. With enormous application and effort, Krishna Raj enlarged the readership of the *EPW* as an international journal of repute. The combination of current comments with well-researched special articles that *EW* had started helped greatly. The *EPW* kept it up and under Krishna Raj's leadership, a series of special articles on agriculture, industry, and management, women's studies and so on were published. The range of articles was enlarged and combined with comments on current world affairs. New features, such discussions on published articles were added. Before his death in early 2004, Krishna Raj had given the *EPW* a worldwide reputation as a journal of importance. The present editor, C Rammanohar Reddy, who took over editorial responsibilities later in 2004, has in the last few years further enhanced its reputation, reach and influence. He has regularised the web edition and added several new features. As of now, one is reasonably assured of its continuance as a publication of world standard.

My relationship with the journal changed somewhat after my shift to Bangalore. Not being engaged in any macro policy after leaving the RBI, I refrained from commenting on monetary or banking policy, lest my comments were misinterpreted by those continuing in the RBI. It would also not have been wise to do so as I was not privy to the wealth of data flowing into the Bank, or the inner processes of decision-making. My links with the *EPW* changed into one of trusteeship rather than of a confidant of the editor or his staff. When Krishna Raj died in 2004, I was chairman of the Sameeksha Trust and together with the managing trustee had to choose his successor. Thanks to the wise counsel provided by many who had seen him develop, we could persuade Rammanohar Reddy to take over as the journal's editor – a decision of which the trustees are happy and proud.

NOTE

1 For a fuller account of this, see *The Reserve Bank of India*, Vol 2 (1951-1967) pp 715-721.

A Final Word

A word before I sign off. It is not vanity or a sense of self-importance which has made me write these memoirs. It just happened that by the time I finished my education, momentous events were happening in India and those of us fortunate enough to be young and active at that juncture had immense opportunities in a new, development-minded country. In the preceding pages, it has been my endeavour to set out the kinds of issues which I and others like me had to deal with one way or the other. We were led by men of great vision and political experience; and in the course of our journey through life we found it possible to go places. We could play our little part in different kinds of nation-building activities of a nascent administration. Looking back on the past half-century, I have often been faced with two interrelated questions – were the policy decisions then taken the right ones for those times; and in today's changed situation, what is my assessment of those policies? Decisions taken in the RBI were not like those of the PC; one was concerned mainly with monetary policy while the other had wider developmental responsibilities. My comments will first cover the macroeconomic development policies. I shall come to the RBI after that.

After achieving independence, India's primary interest was in development, to raise per capita incomes as fast as possible and reform the economic and social structures. Prime Minister Nehru was very keen that India should quickly become industrialised and technologically progressive. Consequently, the first perspective programme dealt with the "big push" to industrialise under state or government auspices. Since India was short on capital but rich in labour, this programme required a progressive increase in domestic savings, import of foreign savings as available and utilising labour resources more efficiently to add to the stock of capital assets. This perspective plan took clearer shape in the Second and Third Five-Year Plans.

There were three aspects to this perspective plan which were hotly debated. First, was this strategy of development right or manageable? Second, was it necessary for government to occupy the "commanding heights" and impose a barrage of controls on private enterprise? And three, was it naïve to assume that this strategy would add to both production and employment of labour? The Plan schemes, collectively called the "Nehru doctrine", have been much debated in India as well as among development economists everywhere.

Two issues dominated both public and professional discussions at that stage. One related to the massive investment by the state on basic and capital goods industries and the other to deficit financing for development. Regarding the latter I have already said my piece in Chapter 2. As for the "big push" theory, one cannot say what could have been achieved had Chinese incursions and wars with Pakistan not interrupted the five-year plans so disastrously in the 1960s. I still believe that had the government concluded the Third Plan and gone on to the Fourth Plan in sequence, we would not be facing the infrastructural bottlenecks we now face. How this may have affected both fiscal policy and agriculture is a different story. We might still have had to have the "green" and "white" revolutions to benefit the rural sectors. But I doubt that rural employment would have benefited except in Punjab, Haryana, Gujarat and a few others. In all of them, improved seeds, multiple cropping, and additional fertilisers and pesticides became available and other land-based enterprises developed. But it remains that the big lacunae in the 1960s were the inadequate attention paid to education, public health and social security in the Third Plan and the draft Fourth Plan prepared when Nehru was alive. With his death, and that of Prime Minister Shastri later, things went haywire. The result was continued deprivation of these basic facilities to the rural population. Not that the so-called Nehru doctrine ignored these altogether. But inadequate provisions for them have resulted in the present poor supply of a skilled and well-nourished labour force. Administrative inefficiency and corruption have exploited the public so much that wealth, incomes and political powers have been grossly maldistributed.

Aspects such as a misplaced emphasis on small industry, the brain drain, ineffective civic organisations and the growing concentration of authority in the central government have all been wrongly blamed on the PC and the Nehru doctrine. But the strategic failure was basically in the lack of adequate attention to the needs of the people, especially in rural areas. These are now sought to be remedied in various ways: through the National Rural Employment Guarantee Scheme (NREGS), Sarva Shiksha Abhiyan (SSA), the National Health Insurance Scheme (NHIS), and so on. But considerable scepticism about all these exists, largely due to administrative deficiencies.

Other hotly debated issues were regarding import substitution versus export promotion and the barrage of controls and regulations on private enterprise. It was during Indira Gandhi's regime in the 1970s that controls become rampant. Since then, many of them have been eased or removed altogether with the 1991 reforms and globalisation of Indian trade and industries. As a result there has been a significant growth of exports as well as a sizeable accumulation of foreign reserves.

The really controversial issue was that of the barrage of controls and regulations on private enterprise. While in the 1950s, even the Bombay Plan argued for state leadership in developing the manufacturing sector, the position changed in later decades. The corporate sector desired to be taxed less and provided more freedom to borrow abroad, as well as engage in new industrial enterprises, often in partnership with foreign companies. The latter were also eager to enter the Indian market. The plethora of controls limiting free access of private companies to real resources was much resented. Besides creating mutual suspicion between the public and private sectors, they came to take adversarial positions, resulting in black markets of all types. Far from being a productive relationship between the two sectors, this caused much friction and ill-will, and greatly reduced the efficiency of public administration. It is only since the 1991 reforms that sectoral relations have improved. But administrative inefficiencies continue to hamper progress.

On whether the policy decisions taken by the PC were right or not in my assessment now, I have only a few observations. I have already referred to the neglect of education and health investments, and their consequences to general well-being as also labour efficiency. Additionally, two other issues should be noted. First, there has been a remarkable growth in both domestic savings and capital formation. From the guesstimate of domestic savings of 5 to 6 per cent of GDP in the 1950s, it had gone up to as much as 35 per cent in 2007-08 and gross domestic capital formation to nearly 36 per cent. The expectation then was that as more domestic income was generated, more savings and investment would be possible. But we did not then expect that India could really save as much as a third of its GDP. This may be a consequence of worsening income inequalities; the Prime Minister Manmohan Singh hopes to remedy this through "inclusive growth policies". What exactly this means is not clear.

The other policy matter on which we may have been misguided was that relating to import substitution. We probably overestimated the effectiveness of this policy in facilitating industrialisation. Apart from imposing many controls on the private sector, we laid undue stress on the possible linkage effects of public enterprises. This did not happen and it was only later, when I was in the RBI, that I realised the importance of facilitating India's exports. In the initial stages, however, additions to industrial production were expected to reduce India's dependence on imports. How different things might have been had we opted for more exports *and* more imports can only be speculated now. Altogether, I do not believe that we could have done anything different in the 1950s and 1960s. We may have been wrong in hoping that the political climate and administrative efficiency would remain what they were in the early 1950s. Changes in these have been more than a little, as is now clear.

Turning to the RBI's policy decisions, there really is not much to add to my observations on their need then or now. I believe that we did right to guarantee commercial bank lending to small-scale businesses. I also think that reducing the cost of credit to exporters has helped the export sector. But the CAS was ill-conceived. We could have done better to set "prudence" criteria for commercial banks on permissible capital adequacy and risk asset ratios, especially in respect of large or long-term loans.

There were, however, two questions the RBI had to deal with frequently. One related to government borrowing in the capital market, and the other to the interplay between fiscal and monetary policies. From the viewpoint of the RBI, over-borrowing by the central or state governments would amount to "crowding out" the private sector's access to the capital market. It was on this issue that I had differed with Governor I G Patel in 1978. My argument then was that larger borrowing by the government would inevitably lead to forcing others to borrow at higher rates of interest; this would have rendered the Bank's administration of commercial bank interest rates difficult, especially when higher public spending could not be offset by a corresponding reduction in private expenditure. As expected, commercial bank lending rates moved up as the government's draft on the capital market increased during the 1980s. But in today's changed circumstances, when we are dealing with recession everywhere, massive public borrowing for current or capital expenditure could be helpful. It is only necessary to watch when to go the other way. I see no reason to think otherwise now.

The more perplexing question was the interaction between monetary and fiscal policies in the context of development. The RBI has to decide exactly where it should draw the line between holding the price level and facilitating additional resource mobilisation for more domestic investment. It clearly had the responsibility for intermediation – that is, promoting additional savings for additional investment, public or private. Through adjustments in the SLR it could always facilitate borrowing by governments, without increases in aggregate deposit receipts of banks. These latter were, in their turn, a function of extension of banking facilities, level of deposit rates and a community's preference for holding liquid resources. With its limited means for controlling money supply or credit expansion, the RBI was often in a dilemma on what to do, when government budgets went into a major deficit and had to borrow either from it or from the market. As mentioned earlier, it is not possible to stop the central government from borrowing from the Bank nor can it offset government recourse to the open market by other means.

At the Bank's management level, we had often to decide policies on hunches about what the likely budget deficit would be, after the government had spent its tax and other revenues and borrowing to meet shortfalls in aggregate resources. What is budgeted is not always what is actually spent; it could be more or less, depending on what it exactly proposes to achieve. For instance, the (2009-10) budget was based on both a higher primary deficit and massive public borrowing. How much of this actually gets done over the year can only be estimated. Only the future will reveal the actual current and capital expenditures. One cannot forecast whose expectations will go awry, whether the Finance Minister's or the RBI governor's.

These memoirs are principally to clarify to myself why certain things needed to be done in the situation prevailing then. It is not meant to be a historical record but only of events to which I was witness. What might have been appropriate 50 or 60 years ago may not be relevant today. But a sense of historical processes often helps in appreciating the social change that has occurred since. If it helps in clarifying why certain decisions taken decades ago have contributed to India's transformation, I shall be more than happy.

APPENDIX I

Thoughts on Inflation and Distribution*

WHEN about this time last year professor Bhabatosh Datta informed me of my election as president of the Indian Economic Association for 1976, I naturally felt greatly honoured. I also felt a little embarrassed because the honour conferred on me was out of proportion to my contribution to the association's activities in the past years. However, I was grateful for the generosity extended to me and I should like to express my sincere thanks for affording me this privilege. I am also glad that this conference is being held on the occasion of the Diamond Jubilee celebrations of the University of Mysore. It is in this university that very many years ago I started my career as an economist and I am particularly happy that we are meeting under the auspices of my alma mater.

I should start with a disclaimer. My predecessors in this position have generally been men of great learning and wisdom. They have, each in his own way, specialised in particular branches of economics and made significant contributions to either analysis or policy. Many of them have advised the government, chaired important committees or commissions, and represented the country in international agencies or conferences with great distinction. Unlike them, I do not lay claim to having made deep research in this or that particular field. I cannot speak with authority on any of the subjects which are normally the concern of economists, though I have had occasion to delve into some of them in the several jobs to which I have been assigned from time to time. In short, I am a general economist; or, as one of my friends used to say, a "memorandum economist", inasmuch as the bulk of my activity has consisted of preparing memoranda for the benefit of policymakers. If, therefore, you find my talk to you today less erudite than you expect a presidential address to be, do not complain that you were not forewarned.

* Presidential Address to the 59th Annual Conference of the Indian Economic Association, 28 December 1976.

Over the last 25 years during which I have worked as an economist in the public sector, I have been associated mainly with matters connected with development planning and monetary policy. In both these areas, these past two decades have witnessed a great deal of development in the Indian economy – significant growth in the national product, diversification of economic activity, creation of national markets, adoption of modern technology over wide areas, attainment of higher standards of public health and technical skills and many more notable achievements. In the immediate past, much success has been achieved in combating inflation and in developing exports. To all these achievements, members of my profession have contributed significantly and we might derive considerable satisfaction from that knowledge. Yet, despite all this, one cannot help feeling that, while many battles may have been won, the war is far from having been won. Poverty, unemployment and malnutrition have yet to be banished from the country. We have a very long way to go before we can even speak of full employment at a reasonable standard of living. We have yet to find a way of maintaining continuous development without domestic inflation, payments imbalance and social or political instability. These are challenges not only to the politician and the administrator, but equally to the economist and the social scientist.

In pondering over these matters, the economist has to recognise that the problems to be solved are related to particular historical contexts. I make this obvious point for the reason that, in the process of evolving workable solutions, it is inevitable that we should make many simplifications and assumptions. While doing so, we create schemes or models which need not necessarily reflect the prevalent reality fully. And having evolved model solutions, we are apt to overlook the difficulties of clearly establishing the identity between the logical scheme and the specific problem on hand. Even when care is taken to avoid oversimplification of the real world, the solutions we evolve cannot always be given a clear-cut time profile or a precise quantitative measure. Admittedly, more or less of such divergence from reality is inevitable for the reason that not all facts can be known at once or measured with equal facility; and even if that were so, not all of them are necessarily reconcilable. While economists may be aware of these limitations when recommending prescriptions or policies, those who implement such policies often fail to appreciate the reservations if the results indicated are broadly acceptable to them. The risk of such blind acceptance is often enhanced by the fact that both the policymaker and the economist are likely to view things from their particular cultural standpoints. They are then liable to minimise or ignore the limitations readily. It is also possible that they act without any knowledge of the enormity of institutional or motivational change which a solution subsumes. These risks are particularly great when change, no matter what it is or what it is for, becomes in itself a desired objective of policy. Under such conditions, the economist who seeks to advise the policymaker has to exercise great care and forbearance in suggesting solutions to the nation's problems. If they do not do so, they may end up as apologists and propagandists for some group rather than as scientists concerned with the interests of society as a whole.

Lest there be any misunderstanding, I should add that there are many in such positions who have tendered honest advice, maintained fully their intellectual integrity and earned the respect of the laity and the professional alike. My intention is essentially to bring out the need for greater objectivity and caution in providing solutions to the many economic problems that we face. If I have been more explicit in the case of the economist, it is only because I am one of them and, therefore am better aware of the pressures to which they are subject.

Since, as I said earlier, my own involvements in the past have been in the areas of development planning and monetary policy, I have had the opportunity to watch closely the conflicting elements that have to be reconciled in the process of decision-making in these areas. It is not possible—nor would it be interesting—to comment on all of them. However, during the rest of my address, I should like to dwell on two elements which have recurred over the years, namely, the questions of price inflation and of distributive justice. I should like to offer some random thoughts on these for the further reason that, in my judgment, they have become as much matters of political friction as of economic analysis.

There is perhaps more public debate on the question of prices than on any other issue these days, not only in India but the world over. This is not surprising, since, depending on what side of transactions he is on, everybody finds his welfare adversely or beneficially affected by a movement in one or more prices. When groups of people are so involved, there is obviously a conflict of mutual interests arising from the effect of price changes on money incomes, output, distribution of real income, balance of payments and so forth. It becomes inevitable for each social group and for the government to take a position on this issue, and economists are naturally drawn into the fray.

There is of course no question that a large and continuous rise in the general price level is injurious to the social interest, both in terms of current welfare and future development. However, it is not always clear at what point price movements cease to curb demand or elicit the additional supplies desired by the community. In principle, output becomes inelastic to price or demand increases at the point of full employment of one or the other of the factors of production. This of course is tautological, since there is often no way of identifying the point of full employment except in terms of price increases accompanying demand increases. There is implicit in all this the assumption that commodity or factor substitution at the margin has ceased to be a possibility for technological or structural reasons. Consequently, the position one takes on price changes in any particular context depends on a variety of judgments not only on the prevailing technological and structural factors, but also on the desirability of a change in them.

Since in reality prices do not change all at once, a series of adjustments in relative prices will have occurred before the overall price index shows a perceptible rise. Such changes in relative prices are generally likely to be accepted as useful, unless the distributive effects are socially disruptive and there is little or no evidence of increase in output or employment. Indeed, under conditions of administered prices, relative price changes are effected for achieving these very objectives; price increases of particular commodities are viewed as incentives to additional production or investment and hence to additional employment. That in the meantime the terms of trade between two groups alter for the worse for one of them is either ignored or considered worthwhile. If relative price changes caused resource and demand shifts to occur in such a way that no bottlenecks arose, no particular group need be affected seriously or for long. On the basis of an increased real product, countervailing measures in the shape of fiscal transfers could, if necessary, be adopted to mollify the aggrieved sections. But if bottlenecks in production or supply intervene and there is an accumulation of prices and costs, efforts to counter this situation through fiscal measures may lead to further price increases. Lags in the adjustment of output and expenditures to higher prices further complicate the matter.

I have referred to these commonplaces in economics because they get blurred in public debate, especially when such debate is between interested groups. As we all know, in the last few years when there has been a great upsurge in prices, there have also been significant shifts in terms of trade between food and non-food articles, between agricultural products and manufactured goods, between wage goods and investment goods. In each of these phases, there have simultaneously been demands for curbing inflation, providing price incentives for additional production and neutralising the price changes through compensatory policies. In general, wage earners and fixed-income earners have pressed for anti-inflationary policies – particularly in terms of overall monetary and fiscal measures – while the agricultural, trading and manufacturing sectors have sought specific price and profit incentives in the name of additional production and employment. Both arguments have been plausible; the dispute has, as may be expected, been about the measure in which each of them is right in any particular context.

When price increases were very large, it became the fashion to focus on the demand factors of the economy as the leading factor in inflation. This is true not only of economists but of politicians and businessmen as well. They all campaigned for measures to curb money supply through cuts in monetary spending by one or the other sectors of the economy. Reduction in government expenditure, curbs on spending by the upper-income earners, taxation of agricultural incomes, wage, salary and profit freezes – all these were advocated with greater or less emphasis by different interested groups. Despite many differences, there seemed to be, however, general agreement that, unless increases in money supply were strictly limited, other anti-inflationary policies would have little or no effect. This had of course the appeal of simplicity and perhaps of equity in a superficial sense, in that the cuts in expenditure were mooted in terms of aggregates and in terms of rates of increase. It was only when those who had to implement policies probed into operational details that the remedies lost their appeal or even became unpalatable because of their impact on other objectives of economic policy.

Let me elaborate a little on this. Leaving aside eccentric remedies, the most common prescription recommended to the government and the monetary authorities has been to assign the primary role in price variations to money supply with the public. Typically, the argument has taken the form of identifying a "safe" rate of increase in money supply or in deficit financing by the government or in credit expansion by the banking system. This would naturally be based on assumptions regarding expected growth in the national product, likely amount of import surplus and constancy over a period of economic parameters defining the behaviour patterns in the system. Occasionally the ceteris paribus (other things being equal) conditions would refer explicitly to patterns of distribution or consumption. But these aspects were brought up either separately or as an afterthought rather than as an integral part of the argument.

In the kind of monetary analysis that we have pursued, we have tended to postulate categories broadly corresponding to economic sectors or social groups identified in national accounts or plan programmes. Changes in money supply with the public are related to (i) net borrowing by the government sector, (ii) gross lending to the commercial sector, (iii) net increase in foreign assets (that is to say, net lending to the rest of the world), and finally (iv) net variations in the non-monetary liabilities of the banking system. Each of these sectors, namely, the government, the commercial entities and the rest of the world is believed to be motivated differently; and if the accommodation each of them seeks from the monetary system is to be adjusted upwards or downwards, different types of instruments will have to be used. It is of course possible to argue that this approach leaves out the motivations and reactions of banking institutions in the economic milieu, and bring in a little bit of money multiplier analysis. But the fact remains that, whether we talk of net bank credit to some sector or increase in high-powered money as a source of monetary expansion, we are still talking in generalities. Before they become meaningful in an operational sense, they have to be dissected into their components and this is when the trouble arises.

Take the government sector. The component associated with it, namely, net bank credit to the government, is a conglomerate of several items. It includes long-term borrowing by the central and state governments from the banking system, absorption of treasury bills by the RBI and commercial banks, and net advances to central and state governments. Since loans to and investments in public-sector corporations are excluded, this element consists of borrowing by "general government" – that is, to say, that part of government concerned with the administrative functions of the governmental system. These functions are not, in principle, related to market operations. In terms of categories, however, it is not exclusively consumption expenditure that belongs here, but also some investment.

Now, each of these elements – market borrowing, floatation of treasury bills, and net advances to government – derives from a different set of judgments or commitments. Long-term borrowing is treated as a non-inflationary source of finance for Plan purposes, on the argument that ultimately it amounts to absorption of the savings of households via the financial institutions. Consequently, it is accepted that the objective of policy should be to maximise it. When this course is followed, there will formally be an increase in the accounting measure of net credit to the government sector and one is then apt to argue that a major factor causing increases in money supply is government borrowing from the banking system.

This pitfall has been well recognised and attempts are made nowadays to segregate what may be called "pure" deficit financing by the government. This is defined generally as the increase in government's floating debt (that is, treasury bills) plus net loans and advances to "general government". Since commercial banks do not provide short-term credit facilities to the central or state governments, and since generally treasury bill holdings of commercial banks are limited, it is also the practice to judge "pure" deficit financing by the extent of net RBI credit to the government. This includes, however, the additions to RBI's holdings of rupee securities attributable to its open market operations. In other words, its size as now measured depends not only on a variety of decisions taken within the government proper, but also in the Reserve Bank on macroeconomic considerations. It is apparent that a different kind of judgment than that pertaining to purely governmental functions could operate here.

Allowing for minor adjustments, it seems legitimate to focus on RBI credit to government as indicative of the additional liquidity generated to enable the government to carry out its commitments within any given period. On the plea that it is injurious to price stability, many economists have argued for minimisation, if not elimination, of this element from the government budget. Virtually all businessmen have endorsed it, more with a view to limiting the scope of the public sector than for any other consideration. There have of course been occasions on which those in the private sector have favoured deficit spending by the government as a means of creating additional demand for industries faced with sluggish markets. That apart, the general view at this point of time is that the less deficit financing there is, the better it is for the economy; and this tenet has been strongly adopted by the expenditure controllers in government. However, as against the expenditure controllers, those in charge of government programmes of various kinds will be focusing on the real objectives which they are enjoined to achieve, and their pull will understandably be in the direction of overachieving the targets. When these interests collide, the outcome depends on the distribution of political power within the government rather than on any economic logic. When it appears politically expedient to press ahead with certain programmes of investment or mass welfare, the expenditure controllers' first gambit will usually be to try to impose cuts on non-priority or non-productive items of expenditure in the government budget, or to seek a transfer of resources from the non-governmental sector to the budget. Trimming non-productive expenditure often involves having to dispense with transfer payments, cut back on interest paid on government borrowing, reduce expenditures on defence and administrative services, and so forth. In all these areas there may undeniably be room for economising in various ways. But since these economies are required to be attained without affecting employment, reducing subsidies, curtailing the services and so forth, the budget-makers may have little scope to operate. In other words, the curtailment of any part of government expenditure will be resisted on the ground that it leads to deprivation of income or benefit to some part of the community or other. And depending on their social or political backing, these cuts become or cease to be practicable propositions.

Since no ministry or department in government will accept that any part of its spending is wasteful, the attempts at cutting non-productive expenditure in the past have usually ended in minor changes in provisions for stationery and printing, travelling allowances and such inconsequential items. Not unexpectedly, those in charge of budget operations have sought to impose their cuts elsewhere, and this has inevitably been in the shape of reducing development outlays. They have been able to do so for two reasons: first, these are expenditures which have yet to be incurred and, therefore, it can be argued that there is no obvious denial of jobs or income to any of those who may be presently occupied. It is in respect of future jobs and future benefits that the decisions have to be taken; and these are more easily taken, since future costs and problems may be highlighted sufficiently to make the cuts appear on balance socially beneficial. The second and perhaps more important reason is that, as budget deficits become large and prices rise, the development lobby finds itself weakened by the onslaughts of middle and higher-income groups which have vested interests in the status quo and in limiting public sector involvement in investment and trading activities. The conflict between these elements is as real and potent within the government as it is among academicians or politicians. Projects or programmes yielding benefit over a period, as well as those that contribute to an improvement in the quality of life – such as education, health and environmental improvements – are postponed, if not abandoned. While this may be a smart thing to do in terms of demand management, it has clearly the effect of perpetuating patterns of production and demand in their existing moulds. It protects, in other words, the prevailing power structure in society from having to yield place or accept unpalatable adjustments. Indian experience of the last two decades is replete with "remedies" of this kind.

There is of course a point beyond which this cannot be pushed in a development-hungry country like India. When this point is reached, and the budget controllers discover that the "saving" in expenditure is also prospective, they have sought to cover their flanks by seeking additional resources for the government, particularly in the form of shifting budgetary items of expenditure to financial institutions and/or appropriating a larger part of commercial bank resources through sale of more long-term securities to them. As is well known, the statutory obligation of commercial banks to hold government securities has steadily gone up over the last few years; this has not always been with a view to reducing the RBI's holding of such securities, in which case it would have been a pure and simple monetary operation. The objective has rather been to put the government in possession of more funds for expenditure during the year.

It will thus be seen that because of the multiplicity of governmental objectives – and the diversity of interests within the government – there is or can be no precise relationship between economic achievement and the budgetary outcome. Much the same type of problem arises in the area of credit to the commercial sector. This is a grab-bag, including mammoth public enterprises, large and medium-sized productive units in the private sector, small-scale industries, wholesale and retail trade, agriculture, professions, so on and so forth. Furthermore, the needs of these are met by a large number of independent institutions, each of which has its own ethos and interests to satisfy. Much more relevantly, each of the banks – or banks' management – has to take cognisance of the social and political impact of their decisions on the community in which they live and work. It would be unrealistic to expect them to take a completely objective view of things, or stand up to pressures of all sorts regardless of consequences. Indeed, they have to be more or less than human to be totally impervious to anything but a formula or a guideline. Within the policy framework set by the RBI, the management of any individual bank has to apply it to each case, and assign weights to each of the elements entering into the assessment. Even when the guidelines are clear-cut and simple, it is inevitable that individual decisions should deviate from the norm. And when this happens to run counter to the interests of a politically powerful section, the bank runs the risk of being adjudged unfairly.

The trouble is compounded by the fact that, with monetary policy having to serve a multiplicity of ends, the guidelines are never simple and few. When credit expansion in the economy is to be limited, there is always a proviso attached – namely, that credit control or restraint should operate in such a way as not to inhibit additional production or additional investment in this or that essential sector. Food procurement, exports, agriculture, small industries, vulnerable sections, core industries – all these become, each on its own logic, a priority claimant on banks' resources. On top of it all, on grounds of preventing sickness in industry or avoiding displacement of labour or alleviating deprivation under scarcity or drought conditions, further demands are made on the banking system. Individually, none of these items can be considered unworthy of support in our conditions; but in the aggregate they leave the banker with no choice but to deviate from one or more of the directives that may have been issued on the basis of macro-economic balance.

This inherent difficulty in applying scarce credit to alternative uses is complicated by two further elements. As I have already mentioned, when they are hard-pressed, budget-makers find it advantageous to shift the pressure on to the banking system. One way of doing it, as already mentioned, is to seek direct support for government spending from banks' investment portfolio. When this indirect pressure is fully exploited, additional spending by the government is sought to be countervailed by requiring a curtailment of bank credit to the private sector. However, since big industry, small-scale industry, agriculture and so forth claim immunity as productive sectors – and each of these sectors has plenty of political clout – there is again a search for dispensable borrowers. For the most part, the candidate elected for this purpose is the trading sector on the ground that this sector is unproductive and given to rigging the market at the slightest provocation. There has undoubtedly been considerable exploitation of scarcity conditions by traders in India as elsewhere. Hence, it is both legitimate and attractive to require that commercial bank credit be not made available to traders who are prone to use it for speculative stock-building. However, if speculative stock-building is to be obstructed, it is not enough to leave the task to be accomplished through denial of bank credit. Every other monetary asset which can be used to hoard goods at a time of rising prices will have to be controlled; or, alternatively, all trade, especially wholesale trade, should be taken over into the public sector. As long as either of these is not done, trading transactions injurious to the community will be possible and pursued. As has been demonstrated in the last two years, the most effective means of combating speculative trading are partly monetary but mainly administrative.

Moreover, it would not be logical to act as if commercial bank lending to the trading sector can be reduced to zero. No matter how production is organised, goods have to be held in the distributive pipelines by somebody or the other. If private trade is abolished, this function has to be performed either by the producers or by the government trading units. In either case, the means of stockholding have to be found and credit to the private traders will in some measure be necessary. It is not legitimate to turn a blind eye to this social requirement. When therefore pressure is exerted by the budget-makers to withhold credit facilities from some part of the private sector, the reactions tend to be similar to those that are generated in the wake of attempts to reduce non-productive expenditures in government. The outcome in either case tends to be incommensurate with the effort.

Let me turn briefly to another matter, namely, that concerning distributive justice. It is now generally accepted that, unless the benefits of economic growth are more equitably shared, there will be neither social progress nor political stability. The programmes for banishment of poverty, ensuring a minimum standard of living and employment, dispersal of economic power, the habitat movement, all these are manifestations of this desire. Because of their obvious appeal, virtually everybody extends his or her allegiance to such programmes regardless of social or political status. However, it is again not always obvious that the means adopted are consistent with the general objective of social justice; and the reason for this is often the same, an unwillingness to grapple with the dynamics of institutional change.

One of the policies which has been evolved as conducive to both larger output and better distribution is that of price support and procurement operations for farm products. Given the low levels of income of the large mass of agriculturists, there is a palpable case for offering higher support or procurement prices when the crops come to the market. Simultaneously with providing additional income to the farmers, these policies have been favoured on the ground that they prevent food and essential article prices from rising steeply and affecting the agricultural labourers and urban poor adversely. To be consistent with these objectives, the operational arrangements have to be such that they ensure maximum procurement both when the so-called free market prices threaten to rise sharply on account of inadequate supplies, and also when the crop is bountiful and the farmers face very low prices in the primary markets. In actual practice, procurement has been low just when there is a shortfall in production and the need was for maximising regulated distribution, whereas in times of bumper harvests, farm prices have been allowed to fall below the procurement price. In consequence, it is hard to avoid the impression that the benefits from this policy have not accrued fully to the poorer sections of the agricultural or the urban sectors. Taken along with the fiscal and monetary strains imposed on the economic system as a result of food subsidies, low agricultural taxation and limitless credit for food procurement, one is puzzled as to what net benefit has actually been sought and derived. Procurement and buffer-stock policies have a role to play in the achievement of growth and distribution objectives; but it is unlikely that this role will be performed effectively without the establishment of an enduring public distribution network. For known and unknown reasons, implementation in this regard has been far from adequate; and one can only surmise why.

Similarly, during the past decade or so, substantial investments in the private sector have been financed with loans and other assistance provided through public financial institutions. In the more recent past much thought and many policies have been directed towards giving larger incentives to private industrial investment. However, this has not showed up materially in larger employment or larger supplies of essential consumer articles. Nor has there been any reduction in the demand for aid to sick units; there are many which have resorted heavily to borrowing from banks for meeting cash losses. Altogether there is no saying at this point of time as to what the distributional effects of these measures have been or will be, and it is difficult to show that the vulnerable sections in the community have benefited in a relative sense. There is, however, some evidence that in the process some of the resources which might have been mobilised for stepping up development outlays in the public sector have not been so utilised. Otherwise, there is no reason why there should be such accumulation of unsold stocks of steel, coal, fertiliser and so forth. Like the building of food stocks this also has inflated commercial bank lending, with attendant consequences on money supply and current and expected prices in several markets. The question once again arises: what precisely has caused such a combination of ill-assorted consequences?

I have referred to these because in my judgment the lack of resolution of such problems is not due to non-availability of relevant or sophisticated economic analysis. Rather, it is because of implicit and explicit value judgments. Hence it is necessary that the economist keeps in mind a variety of para-economic elements that impinge on operational decisions. At the present juncture there is some danger that an unusually large expansion in money supply with the public or aggregate monetary resources, accompanied by a general increase in prices, will either be unduly played down or unduly played up, depending on one's role in the economic system and one's political or economic ideology. There is undoubtedly need for exercising great restraint but not, in my view, for panic or scare mongering. While the general policy of avoiding cheap credit and moving towards better planning of its use are part of the desiderata, the basic solution to the problem of concurrent price increases and demand inadequacies has to be found elsewhere, namely, in the resolution of conflicts on the plane of objectives and sectional interests. Inflation, in other words, is not so much a monetary as a social phenomenon, and its nemesis has to be sought at a fundamental level, that is, in changes reflected in the socio-economic structure.

APPENDIX II

The Limits of Monetary Policy*

FIVE years ago, in December 1976, I had occasion to express a few thoughts on inflation and distribution in my address to the Indian Economic Association.[1] It was my purpose then to draw attention to certain approaches to monetary policy, in the context of the prevailing budgetary practices, payments situation and political environment. As you may recall, the curbing of inflation was a matter of high concern then, as it is now. For some years prior to 1976, restrictive monetary policy had not only been assiduously practised by the Reserve Bank of India, but had received what I considered to be disproportionate credit for checking price increases. It was not sufficiently appreciated that the turn in domestic prices during the period of the Emergency (1975-76) was the consequence of a multiplicity of factors – severe curbs on trade union activity, punitive action against smuggling and black marketing, adjustments in administered prices, sizeable increases in domestic output and, of course, demand management. In retrospect, one could say that the success achieved at that time arose from a combination of monetary and non-monetary measures. However, as I observed a little while ago, monetary policy had more than its meed of praise. An increase in wholesale prices between April 1976 and March 1977 did little to change this general impression.

One concomitant of this has been an increasing shift among policymakers – and, of course, economists – towards monetarism. Changes in M_1 and M_3 tended to become topics of general interest, and when, during the Janata Lok Dal interregnum, industrial output remained stagnant, not only industrialists and traders but virtually everybody else urged recourse to easy money as a means of redress. With a view to stimulating the economy, sizeable

* The First Dr D K Shukla Memorial Lecture delivered at the Department of Economics, Maharaja Sayajirao University of Baroda, on 2 December 1981.

budgetary deficits were incurred by the government in the years 1977-79. The Reserve Bank went along with a reduction in interest rates and some easing of credit authorisation procedures. It was, however, cautious enough to maintain its overall quantitative controls on the banking system more or less intact. Provision of more credit for increasing domestic output was widely recommended, especially by the Ministries of Agriculture, Commerce and Industry, together with the interests concerned in the private sector. The argument that credit was not in itself an input received scant respect; and as the size and range of the nationalised banking sector grew, elaborate targets for output and exports were set on the basis of additional commercial bank credit. It is part of history now that the net effect of this exercise in relatively easy money in the period 1977-79 was not so much an increase in production as a moderation of recessionary trends, a large increase in money stock and the storing up of future inflation. It is of course true that the failure of monetary policy to elicit additional output during this period, like its "success" during the previous few years, could well have been magnified in the popular mind. Chaos in political affairs and disarray in economic administration – and the accompanying lack of clarity about the objectives of policy, administrative inefficiency, and a general decline in discipline and ethical standards – made any kind of progress in these years virtually impossible. Even so, it has to be recognised that more was asked of monetary policy than it could have delivered even in the absence of these disturbing elements.

The severe decline in the gross domestic product in 1979-80, together with the steep increase in the price of crude oil and other imports, brought inflation back with a bang – and with it a renewal of the demand for curbing money supply. Actual or prospective drafts on food stocks and foreign exchange reserves further underlined the need to follow effective demand management policies. The Reserve Bank severely restricted banks' access to additional funds (both from the RBI and other financial institutions), raised interest rates and brought into operation other measures of credit control. However, experience in the second half of the 1970s had also brought into clearer relief the inadvisability of totally subverting the medium and long-term objectives of economic development to the relatively short-term needs of price stability. Continuing bottlenecks in transport, power and other infrastructure services, shortages of several essential consumer goods, growing pressure on labour markets, rapid increase in the trade deficit, widening income and wealth disparities – all these made it abundantly clear that interruption in the growth process had become serious. In this situation, the Reserve Bank of India had to be wary of going too far in the direction of monetary deflation.

In both the public and private sectors there was increasing support to the argument that stringent credit policies, together with higher interest rates, were not always the best way of beating inflation, since in their view such measures adversely affected both current output and investment in additional capacity creation. In consequence, despite the stringent measures adopted to contain commercial bank credit, money supply continued to increase at a high rate, thanks mainly to large increases in net bank credit to the government. In principle, government outlays under Plans were directly linked to increases in domestic output and hence they were sought to be maintained as a means of fighting inflation and strengthening the export effort. It would thus seem that knowingly or otherwise, demand management policies tended to be circumscribed by what has now gained common currency in economic circles as "supply-side economics".

The turnaround in our balance of payments and foreign exchange reserve positions in the last five years has added a further dimension to the debate on where demand management ends and supply management begins. It is now abundantly clear that, notwithstanding additional efforts to enlarge domestic supplies of energy, our crude oil and petroleum product imports will continue to impose a heavy burden on the balance of payments. Trend increases in capital goods and industrial raw materials imports, as also compensatory imports of one or the other of essential consumer goods – like vegetable oils, foodgrains or sugar – cannot be ruled out. While a longer run solution to this problem is clearly a steady and substantial increase in domestic output and exports, the immediate reaction has been a larger resort to foreign borrowing – the high point of which has been the 5 billion SDR loan from the IMF under its Extended Fund Facility. The sheer size of this transaction, together with the "conditions" attached to its utilisation from year to year, has generated widespread economic and political debate, both in India and outside. Saving the details for later discussion, the IMF loan in brief requires India to achieve structural adjustments in production, imports and exports, within the framework of clearly articulated stabilisation policies. An essential component of stabilisation policies is monetary and credit management; however, the Fund requires that monetary and credit management in this context should not just be a means of keeping the lid on aggregate effective demand but should also be supply-oriented.

We are, in other words, face to face with the necessity of evolving, among others, monetary and fiscal policies which are both demand- and supply-oriented. This is not anything very new; the declared policy of the RBI has all along been one of controlling money and credit supply without prejudice to the needs of additional production and exports. But the fact that from now on, both the performance of the economy from year to year and the effectiveness of monetary and other policies pursued by us will be under IMF surveillance, makes it essential that the authorities should spell out – at least define clearly for their own benefit – what supply or demand effect each set of policy measures is expected to have, and over what time period. Such specification is required because the agreement with the IMF has defined intermediate targets in respect of domestic credit, and performance criteria in respect of import liberalisation, containment of subsidies and so on. These have to be attained – or failure to attain them clearly shown to be due to factors beyond our control – before additional drawings on the loan are made. There is, in all this, a presumption that in the economy certain stimuli or restriction will have certain kinds of effects on demands, supplies and prices within the country, and consequently on India's transactions with the rest of the world. There are indeed several aspects of the agreement with IMF which are – or ought to be – matters of deep concern at the political level. But I shall not go into them here. My purpose today is to ponder over a general question, rather than on the IMF loan as such. And this general question is – in the current situation when both stability and growth depend vitally on effective demand and supply management, what, in fact, are the limits of monetary policy? By limits, I do not necessarily mean quantitative limits, but more importantly, institutional and structural limits. I shall not pretend that this evening I shall do much more than identify the problem more clearly, and provoke some objective discussion on economic policy in general and monetary policy in particular.

* * * * *

To return to the main theme, what in brief are the principal reservations relating to monetary policy? First, the operational variable is ostensibly the quantity of money, but in practice, the monetary authority cannot change it precisely or by fiat. The broader the concept of money used, the more difficult it is to change aggregate money supply within a given time period. Second, as has been already pointed out, the ratio of "money stock" to effective demand, or the income velocity of money, is not constant, nor can changes in it be made with any degree of certainty. Such factors as income distribution, propensities to save or hoard, market differentiations and market imperfections, tax structure, patterns of consumer behaviour and expectations, openness of the economy, all these have an effect on the speed with which the income multiplier operates and influences income velocity. Third, there is no unilateral link between changes in effective demand and changes in prices – since "market supply" even under conditions of overall output inelasticity is variable when expectations are variable. Fourth, the effectiveness of monetary policy, especially as an anti-inflationary measure, depends on wage and price flexibility as well as rational expectations – and is not, as Keynes seemed to imply – independent of these. Fifth, as Keynes indeed pointed out, there is an asymmetry in its operation during periods of excess (aggregate) supply as against excess (aggregate) demand; that is to say, it is probably more effective when there is unutilised productive capacity than when there is unsatisfied demand. And finally, its precise formulation becomes difficult when society has multiple objectives to satisfy – such as price stability and balance of payments viability, growth in productive capacity, reduction in income disparities and achievement of other social values, such as economic independence, technological progress, environmental protection and so forth. This is true of all policies as well; but since monetary policy seems so direct and impartial a way of dealing with prices, policymakers often tend to believe that there is no trade-off between objectives involved in adopting it. It is only subsequently that they realise that it discriminates in actual practice against the weakest and least developed part of the economy. Hence, in the final analysis, it is their interests which are sacrificed when monetary policy is narrowly conceived and rigidly applied.

All these reservations are relevant even in the limited Keynesian context of anti-cyclical policy. Needless to add, they are far more important in the context of economic development and structural change – when multiple objectives are the rule rather than an exception, and the assumption of constancy of economic parameters or expectations is unwarranted. We have to keep these limitations in mind while considering the role of monetary policy in India at present.

* * * * *

A combination of factors – some of which are structural, some institutional and some plainly political – has made it difficult, if not impossible, for the RBI to exercise any decisive control on the components of money supply, or its income velocity. It is a commonplace that what are exclusively instruments of monetary policy – namely, Bank rate adjustment, reserve ratio changes, changes in refinance or rediscount facilities, open market operations and commercial bank credit restrictions – will have a quick and determinate impact on the money stock only if budgetary and balance of payments factors are supportive of the central monetary authority's actions. In India, as elsewhere, this has not always been the case. Given the national security and administrative functions that governments have to discharge, as well as the welfare and development programmes that they have to initiate and maintain, a great part of public expenditure tends to become more or less fixed. Any reduction in these involves a troublesome choice between objectives, or between benefits to particular sections of the community – such as farmers, organised labour, manufacturers or fixed-income workers. Governments in the country have been unwilling to pay the political costs involved in abridging a benefit that has already been extended. Even if they are willing, it is not always easy to decide which objective or what group benefit should be given up. Likewise, tax policy, especially direct tax policy, has posed for the government difficult political choices, and despite the frequency of modifications in rates, direct tax yields have not been particularly elastic with respect to total income. Large-scale tax evasion has further diminished the effectiveness of many imposts. Indirect taxes, which for many years now have been the main sources of government revenues, are at existing levels not only tending to become regressive but are having a cascade effect on costs. Public enterprises have, in the aggregate, failed to impart any strength and flexibility to government revenues, despite a series of increases in the prices of their products. All of this can of course be changed by strong, efficiently and honestly administered measures. But this requires many procedures and practices to be abandoned and many vested interests cut down. Governments have preferred to avoid such hard options and instead drawn more heavily on the banking system – not only to meet the needs of public enterprises but for covering the deficits of "general government" as well.

There is hardly anything that the Reserve Bank can do about this, except advise the government strongly against continuation of the practice of large-scale deficit financing. As you know, almost a third of bank deposits are borrowed by the central and state governments or state-owned agencies, under the 35 per cent statutory liquidity ratio that banks have to maintain.[2] While justification for this is sought in terms of restricting the funds available with banks for short or medium-term advances to the commercial sector, it can hardly be deemed an instrument for limiting government expenditure or money supply with the public. The extent of RBI or commercial banks' holding of treasury bills is, again, a matter of accident rather than design. They depend on the day to day variations in banks' cash position or in the cash balances of the central government with the Reserve Bank. Over the years, however, the increase or decreases in net treasury bills outstanding is a function of the precision with which the estimates of receipts and disbursements have been made. Given the propensity of budget makers to overestimate revenue and underestimate outlays, additions to net government borrowing from the banking system have in actuality been more than what the RBI might have provided in its monetary budgets from year to year.

Since Reserve Bank lending to the government is a prime factor affecting reserve money, it follows that the RBI's hold on reserve money is also slight. More so because the traditional offset to budget deficits, open market operations by the central bank, is virtually non-operative in India. On the contrary, because of over-budgeting by the government of its market borrowing, the

RBI has been obliged to purchase dated government securities year after year, rather than sell them and absorb liquidity. Net foreign assets of the RBI, the other countervailing element, have also risen almost continuously since 1974-75, and it is only since 1980-81 that they are declining fast enough to have a contractible effect. While payments deficits are technically suitable for moderating excess aggregate demand in the economy, they can in practice be sustained over long periods only if foreign savings continue to flow in – and if such inflow is politically acceptable. Obviously, an economy aiming at self-reliant growth cannot accept payments deficits except for brief periods; nor will the international community provide such support, except on very onerous conditions, as we have seen in respect of the IMF, Consortium, or USSR credits.

Since the RBI has no power to impose a ceiling on government borrowing or to incur large and continuous payments deficits, it has to train all its big guns on the remaining factor affecting monetary demand and money supply, commercial bank credit to the commercial sector. It is perhaps correct to say that we have credit policy rather than monetary policy in operation; the objects of control have been the quantity of credit available to the commercial sector, as well as the price at which this is made available. Apart from these overall restraints on lending by banks, the RBI has, from time to time, sought to use purely administrative powers and moral suasion to influence the pattern of credit deployment. Selective credit controls, credit planning, directives on priority-sector credit, the governor's advice to banks from time to time have all been measures of this type. While the RBI has undoubtedly succeeded in curbing undue expansion of total credit and in influencing its pattern, the final impact of credit policy on money supply has, as one would expect, been influenced critically by the extent of deficit financing by the government and the state of the overall balance of payments. I have already touched on these matters and shall turn now to another question. Even in the narrow field of credit policy, what in fact is the extent of control that the RBI can exercise?

* * * * *

As the banking system has grown, and as an increasing part of the community's savings has come to be in the form of bank deposits, it has become part of official policy to encourage banks to mobilise additional deposits in the national interest. It is also a policy pursued by individual banks in their private interest. The larger its deposit base, the greater the confidence amongst the public that it enjoys and the less its dependence on outside sources to cater to the needs of large or numerous borrowers. It has therefore been the internal policy of most banks until recently to use deposit mobilisation as an index of success of a branch, or of the efficiency of its branch managers. Manifestly, the policy of intensive deposit mobilisation will continue in the future also; and since aggregate deposits are strongly correlated to national income, whose rapid growth is the prime objective in all of our Plans, fairly high rates of growth in deposits may be postulated for the coming years. It is, of course, possible to argue that deposit growth in the future will be less fast than in the past, on the basis of greater distributive justice – which also is an important policy objective. But there is little evidence of a tendency towards greater equality in income distribution at present, nor is it necessary that greater income equality should reduce savings in the form of bank deposits. It follows then that aggregate money stock (M3) will grow from year to year at least by the amount of the increase in time deposits of banks – unless, of course, the currency and demand deposit components show a decline.

What in reality are the chances of a decline in these components of money supply? Virtually none, I believe. In the first place, this will require a drastic reduction in budgetary deficits – which, for the reasons I have already mentioned – is quite unlikely. It also means, second, a reduction in the transactions as well as the speculative demands for money, especially currency. This again, is something unlikely to happen as long as inflationary expectations exist and inefficient transport and distribution systems necessitate the holding of large inventories by industry and trade, and the attractions of the black market are allowed to grow unhindered. There has been no year in the last 30 years when M1 (that is, currency plus demand deposits) has fallen, and in the last three years, it has nearly kept pace with the growth in time deposits of banks.

Restricting the access of banks to loanable resources, the main point to be noted is that there will continue to be a rapid accretion to bank deposits, and hence the stiff SLR and Cash Reserve Ratio requirements presently in operation should be expected to continue. I doubt, however, that much further increases in the SLR would be right or useful – unless it can be demonstrated that the transfer of such large resources to the government is, in fact, facilitating the provision of low-cost benefit to the poorer sections of the community. In actuality, much of the interest subsidy to the government gets lost in the persistent increase in the capital-output ratios seen in transport, electricity and other basic sectors. Where products or services are in fact provided at subsidised rates, the benefits accrue to producers, traders or other intermediaries, rather than to the final consumer. Before further transfers of the community's savings are made through increases in the SLR, these matters have to be corrected. Further increase in the SLR will also create problems for banks, in the shape of low returns on their assets. This "private cost" can, however, be accepted if there is a clear "social benefit" in the form of larger production of basic goods and services and genuine subsidisation of consumption by the poorer sections. Otherwise, the measure will amount to wastage of capital; nor will there be any benefit in terms of monetary control, since funds made available to governments in this manner are put back into circulation. It also reduces the ability of the monetary authority to operate its control instruments flexibly, since it would, in practice, be difficult to cut down the SLR, as long as the government's budget is in deficit.

Increase in the Cash Reserve Ratio, however, constitutes a genuine means of immobilising commercial bank deposits, as long as it can be combined with denial or drastic curtailment of refinance and rediscount facilities by the RBI. When there is a good case for the central banking authority to use refinance and rediscount facilities for promoting specific ends – such as encouraging food procurement or export finance, or promoting the practice of bill financing – it is possible to argue that a simultaneous use of higher cash reserve rations and specific refinance or rediscount facilities is a means of influencing the pattern of use of commercial bank resources. But since credit is fungible, a good deal of such reallocation of bank resources is more apparent than real. This is particularly so when non-fulfilment by banks of the Cash Reserve Ratio is neither discovered immediately nor is punishable by punitive measures. Under such conditions, it is difficult to ensure that RBI refinance or rediscount assistance does not provide a net addition to bank resources.

As of now, the SLR and CRR requirements absorb 41 per cent of the total demand and time liabilities of commercial banks, including, from July 1979, participation certificates in the aggregate. Since issue of participation certificates to the LIC, UTI, and so on, as well as Reserve Bank assistance by way of refinance or rediscount of bills are still available, banks are able to operate with a credit-deposit ratio of more than 60 per cent on the average. The question to be decided from time to time is whether this is excessive, adequate or inadequate to meet the working capital requirements of the productive sectors in the economy, and to provide in some measure the medium and long-term credit needed by agriculture, small industry and small business. This is not easy because on two major points, there could be a genuine difference in judgment. (a) First, how exactly are the working capital needs of agriculture, industry, trade and so on determined and who does this? (b) And what is the extent to which working capital requirements should be met by the borrowers themselves? These have been matters of wide and animated debate in 1970s, especially after the implementation of the Tandon Committee Report.[3]

These are large questions and I shall touch on only those aspects which are germane to our discussion here. In enunciating the basis for provision of bank finance to industrial borrowers, the Tandon Committee argued that working capital requirements should be so defined as to prevent "undue" holding of raw material stocks, finished goods or receivables; and for this purpose, suggested certain "norms" for different industrial groups. It also supported the view that borrowers should generally operate on the basis of a current asset-current liabilities ratio of 1.25 to 1, and seek to improve this ratio gradually to 1.33 to 1. This meant, in effect, that borrowers should aim at financing up to 25 per cent of "working capital" from their own or other long-term sources of funds. The latter has since been made a general requirement on the recommendation of the Chore Committee.[4] As is well known, all these stipulations, which have been incorporated in the credit authorisation procedures by the Reserve Bank, have been resisted by the borrowers vehemently as being arbitrary and counter-productive. Borrowers have argued, with considerable justification, that market supplies of both indigenous and imported raw materials are irregular and totally unpredictable. Hence it is unavoidable for producing units in India to hold larger inventories than their counterparts abroad. On the side of sales, they have argued – again with considerable justification – that governments, government agencies, public-sector enterprises and large private-sector enterprises settle their bills only after great delay and this necessitates manufacturers to seek larger working capital. These arguments have been further reinforced by the ongoing inflation in costs and prices, which continuously augment the working capital needs.

Allowing for some exaggeration of the difficulties by borrowers, there is no denying that adjustments have to be made – and are in fact being made – by the RBI and commercial banks in their assessment of advances to be provided, in the light of these institutional elements. It is also true that, while credit should not be allowed in anticipation of price increases, price rises that have already occurred cannot be ignored. Furthermore, past experience has shown that credit restrictions can, in fact, be shifted by large or small borrowers to others – either through delays in payment of bills, or through a cut back in supplier's credit available to purchasers. Bearing all these in mind, it is obvious that any decision on the adequacy or otherwise of commercial bank credit for ensuring full utilisation of existing capacity is inevitably a matter for judgment. It cannot be related to the actual or planned increase in net output in terms of a one-to-one relationship. An increase of 10 per cent in the utilisation of existing capacity might in practice require more or less than 10 per cent credit, depending on all the factors mentioned above.

* * * * *

Let me now turn to the other major instrument of monetary policy, interest rate adjustment. Compared to the early 1970s, we have in India today a considerably higher structure of interest rates. Over the years, a conscious effort has been made to fit the different rates into a somewhat more rational pattern. While certain characteristics – such as the relatively low bond rates, preferential refinance to co-operatives, and lower rates on term loans as against cash credit or bill finance – continue, the structure with regard to both deposit rates and lending rates has been progressively streamlined. Effort has also been made to communicate to the borrower the basic fact that capital is a scarce commodity in India, and that a reasonable price should be paid for investible funds.

We have a regime of administered rather than market-determined interest rates. Since we also have a policy of controlling overall credit supply, problems of compatibility between supply levels and interest rates arise frequently. By and large, the situation at prevailing rates of interest has been one of excess demand for funds rather than an excess supply. Since there is no scope for an explicit adjustment of interest rates by the lending institution, ex post balance between supply and demand in the economy is secured either through actual supply of credit exceeding the planned level, or by means of increases in cost of funds through means other than increase in the nominal rate of interest. These sometimes take the form of higher charges for servicing the account, or for documentation or supervision of the loan; or, alternatively, of transactions for purposes of re-lending at higher rates of interest. While undoubtedly such practices exist, the adjustment has in the main been through a reduction in credit made available at the lower end of the lending rate structure. Until large administrative pressure was applied, there were several banks where lending to the smaller borrowers in the priority sectors was considerably less than the demand by them. Likewise, credit made available by banks to the export sector tended to languish, due among other things, to the relatively low rates of interest payable on pre- and post-shipment credit.

Against this background, there has been no lack of advocates of a stiff increase in interest rates, either directly by the RBI or through the market mechanism to curb excess demand for bank credit. While I have some sympathy with the view that interest rates should be stepped up in times of inflation, I do not think that market-determined rates are the answer. High interest rates curb demand only when investment at these rates are not worthwhile; hence when prevailing expectations are one of continuing increase in prices, interest rates have tended to reach very high levels before they start affecting the overall demand for funds. This is on the assumption that demand for credit is, at some level, interest elastic. If this is not so, as may well be the case when losses are subsidised in one form or another, high interest rates could merely be reflected in higher costs rather than in reduced demand for loans. This is particularly so when bank finance is used for build-up of inventories.

However, it is well known that many borrowers who have little or limited access to commercial bank credit have recourse to trade credits, indigenous bankers or moneylenders and pay much higher rates than are charged by banks. There has been enough evidence before committees appointed by the RBI or the government to indicate that many small borrowers would be willing to pay higher rates of interest, as long as adequate and timely credit is provided. This they are willing to do because the alternative is either the moneylender, whose interest charges are very much higher, or loss of output or abandonment of a project. In other words, as banking facilities are extended and improved higher rates on bank advance is unlikely to reduce the demand for bank credit, as long as there is scope for a shift of the demand for funds from the unorganised bankers to the organised banks. The extension and improvement of the banking system is already part of government policy; and if inflation persists, it is more than probable that, at existing rates of interest, credit demand will outstrip credit supply; and the strain on the administrative controls to restrain bank credit will be heavy. It would in this situation be appropriate for the RBI to seek to ease this strain somewhat through higher interest rates. This does not necessarily mean that the maximum lending rate should be raised to much higher levels; it does require, however, a fair increase in the interest rates at the lower end of the range.

At the same time, I do not think that the Indian money and capital markets are large enough or organised enough to warrant total, or even heavy, dependence on flexible interest rates for adjustments in aggregate demand. This is not just because the government and government-controlled agencies, which are notoriously insensitive to interest charges, are major borrowers from the banking system and financial institutions. Much of business in India is still carried on in the relatively unorganised sector of agriculture, small-scale industry and small business, and sophisticated financial management exists only in some large enterprises. Credit authorisation, scrutiny of accounts by banks, submission of quarterly returns by borrowers, stipulation of inventory norms, are all contributing to an enlargement of this habit, and some increase in the sensitivity of borrowers to increase in interest costs may develop. But we have a long way to go before significant effects on supply or demand for credit follow from small changes in interest rates.

In the final analysis, the effective use of interest rates as a means of monetary adjustment depends not only on the sensitivity of the money market but on the response of supplies and demands in different markets to price and wage-rate variation. If product and factor supplies, and demands are inelastic to changes in prices and wages, interest changes by themselves cannot promote resource reallocation. An inflationary situation is typically one in which some crucial supply – such as the supply of wage goods or of a strategic factor of production – is inelastic in the short run in respect of both income and price changes. However, it is possible that demand is not totally insensitive to price changes, especially if these are substantial and if the buyers cannot shift the higher prices to another market (including the labour market). In practice, this has to be discovered on the basis of trail and error rather than on a priori grounds. Politicians and administrators do not find it easy to accept or quickly correct the errors in policy. It is also embarrassing to policymakers to raise prices in an inflationary situation, when the popular demand is for a reduction in prices, and this makes for delay in decision-making on administered prices. Conversely, in a situation of unemployed resources or unutilised supplies, the proper course of action may in reality be the enlargement of expenditure or demand and not a reduction in prices. Experience in respect of both wages in the organised markets, and of support prices of agricultural products, indicates the practical difficulties of substituting policies of wage and price flexibility for broader measures. It is also a moot point how far such adjustments in wages and prices are consistent with the assurance of minimum income or standards of living to the deprived sections of the community. However, I do not wish to press this point since it is equally debatable whether the alternative, monetary policy, is an apt instrument for achieving a more equitable distribution of the national product. Manifestly, the traditional instruments of monetary policy cannot distinguish between one market and another on welfare considerations. Hence it is only in terms of the impact on aggregate demand and aggregate supply that monetary measures have to be justified. And it is on this criterion that the need for interest rate adjustments also should be decided. That is to say, in our circumstances, upward adjustments in interest rates during periods of inflation should be viewed more as a means of reducing the difficulties of implementing quantitative limits on credit, rather than as a substitute for such limits.

Let me now try to pull together the different threads running through this rather discursive lecture. In the first place, we have to recognise that in India the many objectives that fiscal policy has to achieve greatly limit the scope for a compensatory budget policy under conditions of inflation; and this increases the burden of adjustment falling on monetary policy. However, the control that the Reserve Bank can exercise on the quantity of money in circulation is, for institutional and structural reasons, limited and is more or less confined to restraining the expansion of commercial bank credit to the commercial sector. Here again, since the Reserve Bank has to keep in mind both the demand and supply effects of curtailing bank credit, decisions on levels or growth rates of credit supply have to be tempered by considerations of market rigidities, as well as the special needs of "priority sectors", including exports. On balance, it seems preferable to avoid a further reduction in the permissible credit-deposit ratio of banks – to allow for some flexibility of operation to banks, and to provide for substitution of institutional credit for borrowing from moneylenders and traders. This kind of quantitative control would benefit from support by way of relatively high rather than low interest rates. And by and large, redistributive objectives of policy should be sought through a more efficient use of fiscal measures and a more efficient implementation of development programmes than through unnecessary complications in credit policy.

I should merely add that, given the domestic price and balance of payments situations, the quantitative limits that are part of the "conditions" are neither unjustified nor unexpected. One might differ on whether the specific limits fixed for net bank credit to government and total domestic credit creation are adequate or should have been more or less. But even without the IMF loan, it is indisputable that we would have had some limits on these from year to year, as part of anti-inflationary policy. It does not seem worth quarrelling about these "conditions". It is far more important for us to understand the implications of the IMF credit on how exactly we shall fulfil all the objectives incorporated in the Sixth Plan – especially those relating to minimum levels of consumption, reduction of disparities in income and economic power, modernisation of the economy and limitation of foreign investment. There is room for serious misgiving as to what exactly IMF surveillance will mean and how it will affect the process of policy formulation in India. I earnestly hope that these will be openly debated and clear steps are taken to ensure that, in the process of fighting inflation, our welfare and development programmes are not jettisoned.

NOTES

1 This is a condensed version of the lecture delivered at Baroda. "Thoughts on Inflation and Distribution," presidential address to the Indian Economic Association. Published in RBI Bulletin, December 1976 (see Appendix I).

2 State-owned agencies have, in addition, borrowed from commercial banks in the form of term loans and short-term advances.

3 Report of the Study Group to Frame Guidelines for Follow-up of Bank Credit, RBI 1975.

4 Report of the Working Group to Review the System of Cash Credit, RBI 1979.

APPENDIX III

The Reserve Bank and Government: A Broad-brush Picture

FOR individuals and institutions alike, jubilees are notoriously provocative of sentimental journeys into the past. Sometimes these yield works of art, sometimes works of history, which the principal concerned shares with others. On the occasion of its golden jubilee this year, it was natural for the Reserve Bank to look back on its eventful past, and seek to share it with the rest of the world. The Bank thought it appropriate, moreover, to have such a volume authored by an eminent scholar outside the Reserve Bank, so that the full flavour of its major contributions as a central banking institution could be brought out without any blemish of self-praise or institutional eccentricities. The result is the *Reserve Bank of India: Fifty Years (1935-85)* by E P W da Costa published recently by the Bank. Compared with the earlier history of the bank, da Costa's book is slim, elegantly produced and uncluttered with footnotes or appendices. That, unfortunately, seems to be all that can be said in its favour. As an account of the tremendous life of the RBI in the period 1951 to 1985, it is a great disappointment. However, it is not my intention to evaluate da Costa's book here, but use the opportunity it offers to indulge in a little foray of my own into the Bank's past.

My service with the Reserve Bank in various capacities extended for almost 30 years – from 1952 to 1981 – virtually the same as the period spanned by da Costa's book. These were decades in which India moved fast economically and politically as an independent country. They were years of expectation and triumph, of glory and ignominy, of great hopes and great despairs, of development and stagnation, of scientific achievements and religious bigotry, of heroism and chicanery – and all things else. Like everybody, the Reserve Bank was also a participant in these hectic oscillations and inevitably it emerged in each phase a different animal from before. In terms of structure, functions, ethos or authority, the Bank in the 1980s is totally different from what it was at the time of my joining it in 1952. It is impossible to delineate all these changes in full or strict chronological order, and I shall not be foolhardy to try it here. But there are a few broad and distinct strands of development which seem to me worth noting, and I shall attempt brief thumbnail sketches of these.

Even in the corridors of power of New Delhi, the Reserve Bank enjoyed in the early 1950s a rare reputation for efficiency, integrity and sobriety of judgment. Part of this derived, of course, from the signal contributions the Bank had made under Chintaman Dehmukh's leadership, to work out the financial aspects of the transfer of power after 1947, as well as to the Brettonwoods Conference discussions. But a substantial part also originated from the acceptance of the principle that the central bank of a country should enjoy de facto if not de jure great autonomy in matters of monetary and banking policy. It was believed that, like the Bank of England under Montagn Norman, the Reserve Bank of India should be the undisputed guardian of the nation's currency and banking standards and that in these and other matters, the government should not only not interfere with the RBI but seek advice for its own guidance in other matters.

Conditions were probably unusually favourable for such a relationship between the government and the RBI to flourish in the early 1950s. Though India had embarked on its First Five-Year Plan, such questions as domestic resource mobilisation or foreign exchange allocation had not yet assumed the political or economic significance they were to attain in later Plans. There were only the rudiments of the Indian economic or Indian statistical services in the Government of India, while the Reserve Bank had built up a powerful department of research and statistics. On banking and monetary statistics, balance of payments, rural debt, investment and credit, budgetary analysis and so on, the Bank's publications had a clarity and authority that elicited respect. Above all, there was in the country the general feeling that in any matter requiring honest and efficient supervision or advice one could not do better than rely on the Bank.

Looking back, I believe all this was also a measure of the basic values of democracy, independence, and social justice that characterised political parties, bureaucracy and intelligentsia in that decade. When matters relating to agricultural credit and cooperation had to be set on the right rails, it was to the Reserve Bank and to D R Gadgil, B Venkatappiah, or A D Gorwala that the work was entrusted. When questions of credit to the private industrial sector were to be probed, it was again the Reserve Bank that took the responsibility. So it was in matters of public debt policy, exchange rate policy and the like. And when the decision to "nationalise" the Imperial Bank of India was taken, it took the form of making it a subsidiary of the RBI.

LOSS OF IMPORTANCE

Exactly when, or how, all this changed, it is difficult to pinpoint. But there is little doubt that the gloss began wearing off with the bad blood created between the RBI and the Finance Ministry as a result of the Haridas Mundra affair in 1957. The balance of payments crisis around that time, the Second Plan's emphasis on real as against financial budgeting and the growing power of the Planning Commission also contributed to this trend.

Despite these setbacks, the Bank carried a great deal of weight in New Delhi and elsewhere at the beginning of the 1960s. But that decade witnessed a rapid decline in the Bank's stature and authority. The border conflict with China in 1962, unprecedented drought of the early 1960s, the Indo-Pakistan war of 1965, the devaluation of the rupee in 1966, the break-up of the Congress Party – all contributed to a situation when the conflict between monetary stability and economic development not only became acute, but was dramatically politicised. In the process, the Bank acquired, rightly or wrongly, more and more the image of a conservative, private-sector-oriented, status quo-minded institution. Concepts of social control of banking initiated the move towards erosion of the Bank's authority as the sole monitor of banking practices and institutions, culminating with the nationalisation of 14 major banks in 1969.

NATIONALISATION OF BANKS

Whether this decision to nationalise commercial banks was right or wrong is a separate matter. What is relevant is that with this act, the RBI ceased to be in complete command of the banking industry. A phase of "dyarchy" commenced, accelerating the process of the politicisation and emasculation of the Bank in succeeding years. The march of events in the 1970s is perhaps too well known to require recounting. Suffice it to say that the slide which started in 1969, was arrested neither by the ebb and flow of economic events, nor by the changes in government, nor by the decline in the quality of government administration. The nationalisation of banks in 1969 made bank managements a part of the government bureaucracy. It was, therefore, logical to expect an accretion to the power of the Ministry of Finance, in much the same way as other ministries had gained ascendancy over the managements of public-sector enterprises in other sectors.

During the 1970s, the power struggle extended into the corridors of the Reserve Bank itself. For a while, there was even a subterranean conflict within the ministry on the relative roles of the departments of Economic Affairs and of Banking vis-à-vis the Reserve Bank. But more open was the struggle between the government's Banking Department and the RBI's department of banking operations on a variety of administrative matters. Very quickly, the chairmen and managing directors of banks began travelling more often to Parliament Street and North Block in New Delhi than to Shaheed Bhagat Singh Road in Bombay – and not merely to obtain orders on internal administration.

IMPACT OF EMERGENCY

Where exactly all this would have led in the ordinary course, it is difficult to say. But the Emergency settled once and for all the issue in favour of the government, by force majeure. No doubt was left about who was master, and the long process of requiring the Reserve Bank to seek formally or informally the "approval" of the Government of India on matters of banking administration and policy, including internal administration, was complete. The debate on central bank autonomy had become by 1980 a matter of historical rather than topical interest. The changes brought about by the Emergency in India's political life have been so deep and extensive that it would have been unrealistic to expect the Reserve Bank to remain unaffected. In any event, the thesis that central banks should or can function totally independently of the ruling government is no longer generally accepted in any country. The point therefore is not that the RBI is not an "autonomous" agent, but there is no clear understanding as to where, and in what measure, its authority should generally be respected by the government in the social interest. It is this deliberate fudging of jurisdiction that has adversely affected the capability and moral authority of the RBI and hence its effectiveness.

Concurrently with all this, two other strands in government-Bank relationships are discernible and both these are, I believe, part of the wider currents in political economy. The first of these is in respect of the innovative role of the RBI in the financial sector; and the second relates to the more subtle interactions between monetary and fiscal policy, and between planning and market adjustments. Let me briefly recapitulate these, as I perceive them.

BANKING IN RURAL AREAS

The debate on what are or ought to be the developmental responsibilities of the Reserve Bank is an ancient one. However, from the beginning, the Bank was required to play a crucial role in the promotion of institutional credit for agriculture. The principal instrument for this was to be the cooperative movement, and in the 1950s, the bank provided enormous support to this sector. This took the form not only of concessional finance but, more importantly, of administrative reform and strengthening. It is doubtful if, without the extensive support extended by the Reserve Bank, cooperative credit in India would have reached the levels it has actually attained in the last three decades.

A similar leadership by the Reserve Bank was also apparent in the provision of commercial bank credit to the rural sector. The means in this instance was the State Bank of India, with the Reserve Bank underwriting the costs of such expansion. However, the involvement of commercial banking in rural credit which started with a flourish in the late 1950s did not accelerate in the 1960s, partly because of the changes in the economic climate but mostly because of the lack of interest of other commercial banks in this process. It was really in the 1970s that what may be called ruralisation of commercial banking got going. But by then the mantle of leadership in the banking world had been assumed by the Government of India.

However, the Bank's innovative role in other areas of banking was quite spectacular in the 1960s. Starting with the Credit Guarantee Scheme for the small-scale sector, the bank went on to promote the Deposit Insurance Corporation, Industrial Development Bank of India (IDBI), State Financial Corporations, the Unit Trust of India (UTI) and the Agricultural Refinance and Development Corporation (ARDC). All these functioned under the direct control, or the protective umbrella, of the Reserve Bank. Professional staff, infrastructure facilities, equity capital, loan refinance facilities and so on were also provided by the Bank. Most importantly, it was the Reserve Bank which worked out the basic concepts, organisational pattern, operational criteria and rules and regulations for these institutions and nursed them in the formative period. It is indeed astonishing how much the Reserve Bank could do in the 20 years 1950-70 in the fields of agricultural and industrial credit, capital market, commodity markets, credit guarantee and insurance, exchange control and exchange rate policy, and training and research.

Equally impressive is the speed with which many of these institutions moved away from under the Bank's aegis in the 1970s. The Industrial Finance Corporation of India, in the establishment of which the Reserve Bank had played a crucial role in the initial years of independence, had long ceased to be a part of the Bank's group. In the 1970s, the IDBI, Unit Trust and ARDC quickly became independent of the RBI, though tenuous links existed through the Bank's deputy governors or executive directors sitting on their boards. They became more oriented towards New Delhi, with the line of command flowing directly from the government there to the chief executives. The role of the governor of the RBI in respect of these institutions became peripheral, if not non-existent.

Once again, it is but natural that institutions sponsored by the RBI should sooner or later have become separate. But such a change presumes progress towards operational (and philosophical) freedom; and if the breakaway enables the institution to operate with a greater degree of flexibility than is appropriate to a central banking institution, it is all to the good. However, this is not exactly what happened. While the IDBI and NABARD became independent of the RBI, their subordination to the Ministry of Finance became greater and more overt. In that sense, one has the feeling that a prime consideration for separating them from the RBI was to strengthen the government's hold over them rather than to enlarge their operational freedom.

NEW DELHI'S PERCEPTION OF THE FINANCIAL WORLD

I turn now to my third and last point. The biggest change in the government-Bank relationship in recent years emanates from a change in New Delhi's perception of the financial world. Until the late 1960s, cooperative societies and commercial banks were viewed as convenient agencies for disbursal of credit provided by the RBI or counterpart funds or even budgetary allocations. Two things happened in the late 1960s and early 1970s. Planners and policymakers in government woke up to the fact that domestic savings were flowing increasingly into bank deposits and that financial development was an effective aid to resource mobilisation. Second, a variety of budgetary problems could be reduced or remedied by enlarging the access of government or government enterprises to the deposit resources of commercial banks. These perceptions came at a time when, because of the increase in oil prices, dislocation of international currency markets and general inflation, price inflation in India had also become serious. It was vital that budgetary deficits should be controlled in the interests of price stability, and if this could not be done, it was vital that other steps should be taken to curb the growth in money supply and domestic credit.

PUTTING PRIVATE SECTOR UNDER FINANCIAL CRUNCH

There were other considerations, mundane or partisan, which were operative in the mid-1970s, and which ultimately took the form of putting pressure on the RBI to do two things. First, to adjust the statutory liquidity ratio and its public debt operations in such a way as to enhance greatly the government's share in the capital market; and second, to curb the extension of commercial bank credit to the private sector, especially to the large and medium industries sector. Along with these, the bank was also pressed to provide bank credit for crude oil imports, food procurement, cotton procurement and for the short and medium-term requirements of public sector undertakings. This was over and above the increased support that was to be given to the priority sectors.

Back of all these were the non-economic considerations – the power and patronage that went with control of commercial banks; the almost open stance of some in the Planning Commission and Ministry of Finance that the RBI purposely worked against comprehensive resource planning; even the insinuation that the bank fudged monetary data to aid the private sector. The situation was not helped by the unwillingness of successive governors of the RBI to take a firm position on any matter of policy, or the practice by economic advisers in government of the doctrine of development financing through monetary expansion, offset by disinvestment of food stocks and foreign exchange reserves. In sum, the habit of viewing commercial bank deposits as part and parcel of the consolidated fund of India, or of Plan resources for investment, gained ground rapidly in New Delhi, and virtually all policy was oriented towards subordinating monetary and credit policies to the needs of fiscal convenience. Given the intimate link between budgetary operations and monetary movements in the Indian economy, there was nothing wrong or irrational about the general propositions involved in all this. But what made things unsavoury was the acquisitive character of it all.

As I mentioned at the outset, this is by way of a sentimental journey of my own into the past. May be it is biased because of my participation in some of these events from the side of the Bank. That apart, what I have sought to convey is that in these years so inadequately covered by da Costa in the golden jubilee publication, so much of both substance and style happened. I hope somebody will now delve deeper into these matters and produce a history worthy of that institution.